NAKED GOD

The truth about God exposed

MARTIN AYERS

To Cathy, my wife

Naked God
© Matthias Media 2010

Matthias Media
(St Matthias Press Ltd ACN 067 558 365)
PO Box 225
Kingsford NSW 2032
Australia
Telephone: (02) 9663 1478; international: +61-2-9663-1478
Facsimile: (02) 9663 3265; international: +61-2-9663-3265
Email: info@matthiasmedia.com.au
Internet: www.matthiasmedia.com.au

Matthias Media (USA)
Telephone: 724 964 8152; international: +1-724-964-8152
Facsimile: 724 964 8166; international: +1-724-964-8166
Email: sales@matthiasmedia.com
Internet: www.matthiasmedia.com

Scripture quotations are taken from the HOLY BIBLE, NEW INTERNATIONAL VERSION. Copyright © 1973, 1978, 1984 by International Bible Society. Used by permission.

ISBN 978 1 921441 64 6

Cover design and typesetting by Lankshear Design Pty Ltd.

CONTENTS

PART I

NAKED TRUTH

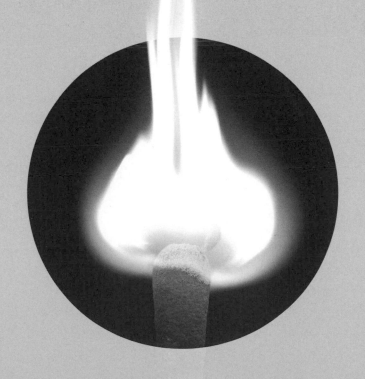

CHAPTER 1

WHY WE NEED THIS BOOK

THE WORLD HAS CHANGED SINCE YOU WOKE UP this morning.

That was how CNN used to advertise their network. It was a fitting slogan for a news channel. If the world hasn't changed, then there's no need to tune in. And CNN had it right. The world is changing. Where do you most notice the change?

When I used to watch CNN, I was living in Beijing. As China prepared to host the Olympics, Beijing was transformed before my eyes. Traditional Chinese single-storey homes were being demolished to make way for skyscrapers. A city that had once been known for its bicycles was struggling with the congestion and exhaust fumes from over three million cars. My colleague recommended I try her favourite restaurant, but within weeks it had been replaced by a new park.

Yet it's not just in China that things are changing. I went to university in 1997. When I visited for my interview, a student there showed me the internet. I'd barely heard of it at the time. In my first year, I queued up with other students at the old red telephone boxes in the market square. Mobile phones were a luxury that few of us could afford. I managed to complete a degree without needing a computer. We still listened to music on cassettes. Technological change can leave you looking dated very quickly.

Our world is changing in other ways too. Let's talk about sex. Do you remember that song? Maybe it was before your time, or maybe it was after your time, but 'Let's talk about sex' hit the charts on my 12th birthday. I remember it well because it was the first time I'd seen a song reported on the national news. Rappers Cheryl 'Salt' James and Sandra 'Pepa' Denton released a song that did something you weren't supposed to do—it talked about sex. Even in the title. It was newsworthy because it seemed so scandalous. Was this allowed? What were the censors thinking?

The strange thing is that looking back now, you wonder what all the fuss was about. If you listen to the music charts today, sex is everywhere. It seems as though almost everyone's singing about it, rapping about it and talking about it. Sex is used to advertise almost anything. Why would a song about sex make it onto the evening news?

But Salt-n-Pepa's song only hit the charts as recently as 1991. The controversy at the time shows us that things are different now. In just a few years, we've grown a lot more relaxed in talking about sex. You might think that's a good thing or you might think it's a bad thing, but either way it's a change.

Change is all around us. It's in the clothes you buy and the music you listen to—if you move with the times. Even the climate is changing, and many scientists warn that our carbon footprints are leading us to a point of irreversible decline.

President Barack Obama ran his 2008 election campaign under the slogan 'Change we need'. In his victory speech at Grant Park, Illinois, he spoke of the change that had taken place in the lifetime of one voter, 106-year-old Ann Nixon Cooper of Atlanta, as part of his rallying cry to the American people to embrace change for the better. He began, "She was born just a generation past slavery; a time when there were no cars on the road or planes in the sky; when someone like her couldn't vote for two reasons—because she was a woman and because of the colour of her skin".

Obama picked out just a few of the landmark changes that had taken place in one lady's lifetime: votes for women, the Great Depression, the Second World War and the African-American Civil Rights Movement. Obama went on, "A man touched down on the moon, a wall came down in Berlin, a world was connected by our own science and imagination. And this year, in this election, she touched her finger to a screen and cast her vote, because after 106 years in America, through the best of times and the darkest of hours, she knows how America can change."[1]

Inspiring words for a changing world. So how do you react to the change that is all around us?

One crucial factor that affects how we feel about change is whether or not we think there is a God. If there is no God, you might think that's a positive thing. You might feel it liberates us, that we're making progress as human beings and changing the world for the better. But on the other hand, it might make you nervous about how the world is changing. Do you worry that the world is spiralling out of control, heading for oblivion as human beings destroy each other and wreck the planet?

If there is a God, it should make us view lots of things differently, including the changing world around us. A greater power than humanity is watching over things. God might still be interested in what happens to the world, and might even be guiding the change we see.

So is there a God or not? Well, here's the problem. That is changing too. Not that the facts themselves are changing, obviously. God doesn't disappear and re-appear again—either there is a God, or there isn't one.

But something is changing. When it comes to the God question, people keep changing their minds. In the 1940s and 1950s, American philosophers developed a growing conviction that there could not be a God. On 8 April 1966, *Time* magazine reported on this by running a cover page that was completely black except for three words in red print: "Is God Dead?" But in the years that followed there was a revolution in the university philosophy departments. So much so that, on 26 December 1969, *Time* magazine ran another question on its front cover: "Is God coming back to life?"

The debate is still going on, and people have been changing what they think. Professor Antony Flew made his name as a committed atheist. He debated against Christians and published books that criticized belief in God. In some ways, he was the Richard Dawkins of his generation. But deep into his retirement, Professor Flew changed his mind. In November 2007, with the help of a co-writer, Professor Flew published a new book entitled *There is a God: How the world's most notorious atheist changed his mind*.

Professor Flew didn't become a Christian, but he stopped being an atheist. His approach was to evaluate the evidence, and on that basis he changed. He decided that the evidence pointed to an intelligent, powerful creator God. Some atheists were so troubled by the news that they suspected Antony Flew had been manipulated or misrepresented in his old age. Flew responded by saying that "My name is on the book and it represents exactly my opinions. I would not have a book issued in my name that I do not 100 per cent agree with."[2] We might not think he's right, but Professor Flew had clearly changed his position.

There are also many examples going the other way, including Christian ministers who have 'lost their faith'. The point is that people's opinions are changing.

When it comes to us deciding whether or not we think there's a God, we can't simply rely on the opinions of 'experts'. We can't let our beliefs be governed by those of a university professor, or our parents, or our peers. We need to examine the evidence about God ourselves, and make up our own minds.

That's what this book is about. It looks at the evidence about God to see what we can uncover. It's about seeing whether we change our minds.

When my mother first told me that she had been enjoying watching *The Naked Chef*, I was a bit alarmed. But I quickly found out that it was a play on words. It wasn't the chef who was naked; it was the food. In his cooking, Jamie Oliver was stripping down the food to its bare essentials.

And that's what we need to do with God. We need to look at the evidence and find out what it uncovers. We need to strip away any false ideas we've developed from our culture or background, and find the truth. This is the truth about God exposed. This is *Naked God*.

Does it really matter?

But maybe you still think this is a waste of time. Even if you have the option of looking at the evidence and working out whether or not God exists, you might still need persuading that this really matters.

I recently met a guy called Simon at a friend's party, and he asked me what I did for a living. At the time I'd stopped being a lawyer and I was working for a church, and he was interested in that. He told me he'd never met anybody at a party before who worked for a church. Simon had just read *The God Delusion*, and he asked me what I thought of it. He said he'd been quite persuaded by some of the arguments Richard Dawkins makes.

It wasn't really the right time to deal with all of the issues in *The God Delusion*, so instead I just picked up on a couple of the major problems others have raised with the book. We had a good discussion, and Simon said he realized that he needed to read *The Dawkins Delusion?* by Alister McGrath, and look into things in a bit more detail.

But then Simon rounded off the conversation with something I found a bit disturbing. He said, "The way I see it now, is that it doesn't really matter whether or not there's a God. If there is a God, then life is amazing because I've been designed and made—and this whole universe has been designed and made—by a master planner. So that's all good. But if there isn't a God, then life is still amazing, because it's just come about by itself. We can't marvel at God anymore, but we can marvel at natural selection and the way that we ourselves and the whole universe have come into existence just by the process of evolution."

I don't know what you think about that. You might just be thinking that this was a pretty full-on conversation to have at a party. I happen to think so too. It seems to come with the job when you work for a church.

But Simon was summarizing a view of life without God that Richard Dawkins argues for in his book. Instead of seeing the universe as something created by God, and standing in awe of its maker, Dawkins says that the universe wasn't created, but that we should stand in awe of its natural causes. He writes that "a quasi-mystical response to nature and the universe is common among scientists and rationalists", and declares that the aspiration of his books is to "touch the nerve-endings of transcendent wonder that religion monopolized in past centuries".[3]

That's where Dawkins hopes his atheism can lead you, and it's where Simon seemed to have followed. People used to think there was a God, and that gave them both a sense of wonder and a sense that they were wonderfully made. But now we've found out that God doesn't really exist. Dawkins proposes a solution to the problem. Behold how amazing science has shown the universe to be. If you can wonder at the universe, why do you need God?

So for Simon, there was no longer any need to work out whether or not God exists. You don't need God to make you feel special. You don't need God to give you a sense of wonder. Therefore, you just don't need God. And if you don't need God, then why do you need to read *Naked God*?

This might be how you think about it too. You might be somebody who doesn't think God exists, and you're getting along fine. Or, more likely if my friends are anything to go by, you might be somebody who isn't sure either way whether or not there's a God, but you don't see what difference it would make anyway.

So the first task of this book is to show why the God question really matters. Before we uncover the truth about God, we need to investigate what life is really like if God does not exist. If things are fine without God, then why bother looking for him?

That's what Part I of this book ('Naked Truth') is about.

In a few short chapters, we're going to look at what it really means for you and me if there is no God. Philosophers have been writing about this for hundreds of years, but we're going to break things down and think about the difference it makes to our everyday lives. What does it mean for our purpose and meaning? What does it mean for freedom? How do we work out what's good and bad? What does it mean for how we approach life and death?

This first section then, is not about whether atheism is true or not. It's an honest look at where atheism leads.

We'll begin by asking the question, "Why are we here?"

CHAPTER 2

NAKED TRUTH ABOUT WHY WE'RE HERE

LET ME SAY AT THE START THAT ATHEISM IS A position of faith or belief just like any religion. That's not meant to be controversial or provocative. It's merely to point out that the statement 'There is no God' is not provable by science or logic. You may have various reasons for believing there is no God, but none of them will constitute a proof as such. At some point, you simply have to put your eggs in a certain basket and say, "Well, if you ask me, there's no such thing as God".

This belief that there is no God is often called 'naturalism'. Naturalism rejects the idea that the universe was created by some sort of God or higher power. Instead, there is actually only one 'thing' in existence. That thing—the only thing that exists—is what we might call 'the cosmos'.

It includes the universe, but there might be more to it than that. Some scientists speculate that there might be a 'multiverse' outside our universe—a place full of lots of different universes. But however far out we have to go, even if it's into a multiverse of some kind, the point is that we'll never find anything beyond the cosmos. There's no other 'thing' out there that caused the cosmos to be here. The cosmos is all there is. Nothing 'supernatural' exists.

And then there's us. We are part of the cosmos. In whatever way the cosmos started, through a Big Bang or something else, it started of its own accord and it's carried on by its own steam ever since. Nothing has interfered, because nothing else exists. Eventually, through the formation of stars and planets and life and a long process of natural selection, we were born. We're made up of the same stuff as everything else in the cosmos.

Under naturalism, it follows on that although humans are extremely complex organisms, we are simply a collection of atoms that has evolved in a certain way. We think, and we relate to each other, and we have what we call 'personalities', but we are all just part of one thing—the only thing that exists. We are matter. We are not designed or made by anyone or anything. We just exist, like a tree or a rock or a polar bear. There is a lot to us, and certainly a lot that we don't yet understand, but it's all entirely natural and physical. It's all just part of the one closed system.

That might sound heavy-going, but it's crucial. Over the next few short chapters, we're going to consider what it means for us in a number of different areas. And the first is in asking why we're here. Is there any meaning to life? It's a question many people are asking.

After graduating from university, my friend Paul landed his dream job as a sports journalist. He became successful and he's a very good writer. But when we went for a drink one night he said to me, "I think that a sense of purposelessness is the curse of our generation". The career is working out for him, but he's still asking, "What is it all for?"

He's certainly not the only one. In December 2006 *The Economist* reported that "affluent countries have not got much happier as they have grown richer". *The Economist* explained that "People are stuck on a treadmill: as they achieve a better standard of living, they become inured to its pleasures … They work hard to afford things they think will make them happy, only to discover the fruits of their labour sour quickly."[4]

In our newspapers, in our conversations with friends and in our own lives, we find this search for meaning in life, for purpose, for fulfilment. Do you ever feel as though you are 'stuck on a treadmill'? Do you ever ask, "Is there more to life than this?"

Often we try to avoid this problem, this sense of purposelessness, by spending our lives trying to attain the things that we hope will give us the fulfilment we need. We focus our energy on a career, or friendships, or a family, or trying to get rich, or creating the perfect home to live in, because we hope these things will give us contentment. If we achieve those goals then we feel settled and fulfilled for a short while, and when that wears off we move on to the next thing.

But it doesn't seem to work. The evidence from those who do achieve their ambitions is that the problem is still there. Paul made it as a journalist, but he's still been left with a feeling of purposelessness. Jack Higgins, the bestselling author of *The Eagle Has Landed*, said that the one thing he knows now that he wishes he had known as a boy is "that when you get to the top, there's nothing there".[5] The danger is that many of us never get to the top, so we never learn.

So how does naturalism answer this search for meaning in our lives? Well, naturalism tells us that we shouldn't even ask the question. We're just collections of atoms in a cosmos full of them. The atoms that make you and me happen to have come together in a way that means we have formed brains, and our brains can think. But the idea that some atoms are more special than others is arbitrary and absurd. We're still just part of the cosmos, and there's nothing more to it than that. Life is meaningless.

Richard Dawkins says:

> In a universe of blind physical forces and genetic
> replication, some people are going to get hurt,
> other people are going to get lucky, and you won't
> find any rhyme or reason in it, nor any justice. The
> universe we observe has precisely the properties
> we should expect if there is, at bottom, no design,
> no purpose, no evil and no good, nothing but blind,
> pitiless indifference. ... DNA neither knows nor
> cares. DNA just is. And we dance to its music.[6]

Without God, the search for a higher meaning to life is futile. If we're victims of a horrible crime, for example, don't bother to ask why. That's just how things are. My friend Paul feels a sense of purposelessness because there *is* no purpose. Jack Higgins found nothing there when he got to the top, because there *is* nothing there or anywhere else. Naturalism leaves us with a void in our lives. No purpose; no meaning; just blind, pitiless indifference.

This might come as a surprise because you might know people, as I do, who don't believe in God yet still live as though their lives have meaning and purpose. But I hope you can see that if you're a naturalist, it doesn't actually make sense to live like that. There isn't any higher meaning to our lives. We might choose a meaning—something to live for. It might be to contribute to society, or to make something of ourselves, or to help make other people happy. We might find that the purpose we choose for ourselves makes us feel more satisfied. But we need to accept that it's just an arbitrary personal choice. There's nothing outside our minds that could say we've chosen the right or the wrong thing to live by.

Before the human race came into existence, there was no meaning to the universe. After the human race dies out, there'll be no meaning to the universe. And while we're here things are no different. All that's going on is that the cosmos currently happens to have arranged itself so that some of its atoms make up complex 'machines' like you and me. We might decide that some ways to live are better than others, but only because our genetic programming makes us think so. You're just one set of atoms, and how that set affects the atoms around them for the next 50 years or so is objectively meaningless.

Richard Dawkins tried to make light of all this in *The God Delusion* by recalling an interview with scientist Jim Watson:

> I conscientiously put it to him that, unlike him and Crick, some people see no conflict between science and religion, because they claim science is about how things work and religion is about what it is all for. Watson retorted: "Well I don't think we're *for* anything. We're just products of evolution. You can say, 'Gee, your life must be pretty bleak if you don't think there's a purpose'. But I'm anticipating having a good lunch." We did have a good lunch, too.[7]

It's a witty response by Jim Watson. But it's also a revealing illustration of the whole problem. Watson doesn't think human beings are anything other than products of evolution. And he's okay with that as long as he has a good lunch. But is that it? Is there really nothing more to life than this? Instinctively we sense there has to be something more, but Watson is just being a consistent naturalist. There's nothing more to life—just get on with making yourself happy, if you personally and arbitrarily decide that happiness is what you're going to pursue. Enjoy your lunch if you can afford one, make yourself comfortable if you can, and don't ask questions about life because this is just how things are.

The naked truth is that if God does not exist, there is no real meaning or purpose for our lives.

CHAPTER 3

NAKED TRUTH ABOUT FREEDOM AND KNOWLEDGE

THE NEXT AREA TO CONSIDER UNDER NATURALISM is what it means for our *freedom*. I take it that we all think our freedom is important. We consider it one of the things that gives us dignity as human beings. People fight for freedom—the right to take decisions without being restricted by others. We want to be free to do what we want to do. We feel that the choices we make are what make us who we are.

But naturalism tells us that we people are not really separate, independently existing 'things' after all. Only one thing exists, and that's the cosmos. When we talk about you or me or somebody else, what we are really doing is splitting down the cosmos into very small parts, and labelling them as separate things. A television, a star, a Ford Focus, a Labrador —these are all collections of atoms within the cosmos.

It follows that if we could know absolutely everything about the cosmos, and trace it through from the beginning, then we'd be able to work out exactly how things have ended up at any given point today. Ever since time began, one thing has caused another, then another, then another, and so on until this certain group of atoms became what they are today.

We can do the same for us. And here's the key: this means that everything about us—every decision we will ever make—has been caused. When we make a decision, we usually think we have exercised a free choice of some kind. But actually, something else is going on. Our decision was partly caused by our nature—the genetic programming we inherited through natural selection. And our decision was also caused by our environment— the circumstances in our life so far, the people who we've encountered, our experiences and what they've taught us. If you knew enough about those causes, you could explain everything. Neitzsche put it like this:

> If one were omniscient, one would be able to
> calculate each individual [human] action in
> advance, each step in the progress of knowledge,
> each error, each act of malice. To be sure, the
> acting man is caught in his illusion of volition;
> if the wheel of the world were to stand still for a

moment and an omniscient calculating mind were there to take advantage of this interruption, he would be able to tell into the farthest future of each being and describe every rut that wheel will roll upon. The acting man's delusion about himself, his assumption that free will exists, is also part of the calculating mechanism.[8]

This is related to the issue we encountered in the last chapter. Naturalism tells us that we're just complex 'machines' within the cosmos. We can't influence the world by our choices, because we're just part of the world ourselves. The naked truth is that we're not free in the way we think we are. We're just part of the system. Even if we can do what we want, 'what we want' is just a product of our genes and our environment. We don't add anything extra ourselves, because there's nothing more to us. If God doesn't exist, freedom is an illusion.

This should have a major impact on how we think about the way we've lived our lives. Have you ever been proud of something you've achieved? Naturalism says, "Don't be". You didn't really achieve anything. You only did what you did because of your genetic programming and environmental influences. If we knew enough about those influences and took them into account, we'd see that everything you did was the product of natural forces (because natural forces are the only forces that exist).

Conversely, it has implications for the way we treat people whom we think have done bad things. If we're appalled by the mind and actions of a rapist or a serial killer, naturalism would remind us that their actions were entirely a product of other causes. If anybody else had been given their identical nature and nurture, they'd have done exactly the same thing.

So if there is no God, and we're just complex machines, is it really right to praise people who do good, or blame people who do wrong? And in our own lives, are we really the free people we want to be?

We end up in a surprising place here. It's surprising because we often think it's *God* who would restrict our freedom, if he exists. Are you put off the idea of a God because you hate the idea of having to answer to him about the way you live? Do you think Christians don't seem to have the freedom that you enjoy? But now we discover that if there isn't a God, we don't have freedom after all. Not in any meaningful sense. We want what we've been programmed to want, and we do what we've been programmed to do. We're just part of the system.

In much the same way, naturalism also undermines our access to *knowledge*. Somewhat paradoxically, when we analyse naturalism by thinking about it, we find out that we can't trust what we're thinking anymore. And of course, if we can't trust our thinking, then we have no way of working out whether or not naturalism is actually true!

It works like this. If we're just a product of natural selection, then that's how our senses were formed as well. It was a process of evolution that developed the way in which we perceive the world around us. Equally, it was a process of evolution that developed the way our minds work, as they process what we observe and draw conclusions. This process of natural selection ensured that we could inherit senses and minds that make us more likely to survive.

But here's the thing—if our senses and our ability to think only came about by natural selection, there's absolutely no guarantee they will actually tell us what is true about the world. Our ability to think rationally has just evolved, like everything else about us. It developed the way it did to help us survive, *but that's very different from saying that it actually helps us to know the truth.* Charles Darwin himself wrote about this problem: "The horrid doubt always arises whether the convictions of man's mind, which has developed from the mind of the lower animals, are of any value or at all trustworthy."[9]

This problem cuts naturalism to its heart. If your mind leads you to believe in naturalism, naturalism then tells you that you can't trust your mind to lead you to the truth. The writer James Sire describes this "ironic paradox", observing that "Naturalism, born in the Age of Enlightenment, was launched on a firm acceptance of the human ability to know. Now naturalists find that they can place no confidence in their knowing."[10]

In this chapter we've uncovered two critical issues that arise if God does not exist. First, our freedom to make decisions is an illusion. Secondly, we can't trust our ability to know anything anymore, including whether or not there is a God.

I realize this might not be how you've thought about

things before, and it might not be how you feel. But what we're doing here is seeing where naturalism actually takes us. It's not pleasant, because it takes us inexorably to conclusions we don't like. But it's only fair to think about the world consistently like this.

Next, we turn our attention to the issue of morality.

CHAPTER 4

NAKED TRUTH ABOUT RIGHT AND WRONG

THERE ARE PEOPLE IN THE WORLD TODAY WHO are doing things that you and I think are wrong. And we think those things are wrong even if the perpetrators themselves disagree. What issues do you care about the most? In no particular order, it might be genocide, or the oppression and marginalization of women, or racial discrimination, or sexual abuse, or destruction of the environment, or military invasions. We all have a conscience, and we all sense that some things are wrong, no matter what the guilty party thinks.

It's not new for people to believe that there is this objective moral standard of right and wrong. But people used to think it came from God. The problem is that if God doesn't exist, we lose the basis for that standard.

Again, we're starting with a view that there is no God, and we're seeing where we end up. We're assuming that the only thing that exists is the cosmos, and nothing else exists to interfere with it. There's nothing out there to provide us with an objective moral compass. It follows that right and wrong are just cultural ideas that have evolved and continue to evolve. Before humans came into existence, no morality existed. And once human beings cease to exist, there won't be any morality either. Values about right and wrong only exist in human minds.

Naturalism here brings us to a conclusion that goes against everything we instinctively know about morality. It tells us that there is in fact no objective scale by which we can measure anybody's actions—all we have are genetically and culturally developed values to which we give the labels 'right' and 'wrong'. When people disagree with us about our values, there's no way of proving that our ideas about good and bad are the correct ones.

Now, this doesn't mean that people who don't believe in God aren't concerned about morality. You might be somebody who currently doesn't believe in God, but you might be a very morally upstanding person. Many people who don't believe in God are the same. They are concerned about society, and about doing the right thing. But the problem isn't that naturalists don't have moral values. It's that naturalists have no basis for those moral values. If you take God out of the picture, you lose your benchmark.

I've talked this over with friends, and some of them have accepted it. However, I think it's worth pausing to consider the objection that a few of them have raised. First, they've said, we all seem to agree broadly about good and bad, so it must be something we've all been born with. And secondly, if people do disagree, then we're happy to think through our moral values and work out what's best for society as a whole.

. This might be what you're thinking as well. But it doesn't solve the problem. For a start, the first part of this argument assumes that, by and large, everyone is born with a similar moral compass. But that's not true. Many people, at various times and in various places, think their ethnic group is superior to others. They think that other racial groups should be discriminated against or even killed, so that society can flourish because it will be filled with people of their own race.

Assuming you think this view is wrong, as I do, how would you argue with those people? You can't appeal to a sense of right and wrong that 'we've all been born with', because they weren't born with the same sense as you were. You might say that their moral compass has been distorted because of the environment in which they were brought up, but they could argue exactly the same for you. You are back where you started, trying to show them that their ideas of right and wrong are incorrect, and that yours are correct, but without any objective basis on which to do so.

The second limb of the argument is that we can all develop and modify our individual moral codes into an agreed code of morality as we try to establish what's best for society or the human race as a whole. If this was the answer, then you could try to reason with somebody that their view of morality is wrong because it doesn't do what's best for society. But this doesn't work, either. We have assumed that there is an objective value—the value of doing what's best for society or the human race. Who says that this is the right value? What if somebody disagrees? What if some people have a completely different view of what constitutes the 'best' for society? And the trouble is that they do.

Naturalism leaves us with no standard of morality outside of human minds. Any attempt to solve this problem requires us to introduce a value of some kind, such as the sanctity of human life, or doing what's best for society as a whole. But we can't do that without asking "Why?" Why have we decided on this absolute value rather than another? Only because our nature and environmental influences have caused us to think that this value is important. It's not really 'true' or 'right'—not in any objective sense.

I was struck by what Richard Dawkins said when he was asked about morality in an interview:

> If somebody used my views to justify a completely self-centred lifestyle, which involved trampling all over other people in any way they chose … I think I would be fairly hard put to it to argue on purely intellectual grounds … I couldn't, ultimately, argue intellectually against somebody who did something I found obnoxious. I think I could finally only say, "Well, in this society you can't get away with it" and call the police.[11]

Do you see the problems with this? It might work when the police are on your side. But it wouldn't be because your view of morality is the right one in any real sense. It would just be because the majority power is enforcing your point of view.

And the real problem is where this can lead. Most naturalists tend to be moral people, but by and large they share similar moral values to the society around them. In the Western world at the moment, for example, that moral compass is still heavily influenced by Christian values. But when naturalists realize that morality is subjective, and when they actually live this out consistently, the consequences can be horrific.

The philosopher Ravi Zacharias recalls his visit to the Nazi death camps of Auschwitz and Birkenhau.[12] The following words of Hitler were hung on a wall: "I freed Germany from the stupid and degrading fallacies of conscience and morality … We will train young people before whom the world will tremble. I want young people capable of violence —imperious, relentless and cruel." When Zacharias searches for an explanation for this "scar on the face of humanity", he quotes Viktor Frankl, himself a survivor of Auschwitz. Frankl writes, "The gas chambers of Auschwitz were the ultimate consequence of the theory that man is nothing but the product of heredity and environment— or, as the Nazis like to say, 'of blood and soil'".[13]

Again, the point here is certainly not that all naturalists end up making moral judgements that you or I would say are wrong, and it's not that naturalists in general are somehow worse behaved than people who believe in God. Ravi Zacharias goes on to explain, "Obviously, there have been others in history who, though denying God, may have chosen for themselves the path of philanthropy. But here is the point. A Stalinist-type choice is one that the philanthropic atheist is hard-pressed to rail against once he or she has, by virtue of atheism, automatically forfeited the right to a moral law … It is *true* that not all antitheists are immoral, but the larger point has been completely missed. Antitheism provides every reason to be immoral and is *bereft of any objective point of reference* with which to condemn any choice."[14]

The ramifications of this are life-changing. Without God, there are no universal human rights. You cannot say there is no God and still say that apartheid was really, objectively wrong. You cannot say there is no God and still say that it is wrong to kill off disabled children. You cannot declare these things to be wrong, because 'right' and 'wrong' do not really exist. There are just things we like and things we do not like, and that is as far as anyone can really go.

I began this chapter by considering the issues on which we think there is a definite right or wrong. What would we say to a society that decided it was okay to marginalize women? What would we say to a society that decided it was okay to sexually abuse certain children? What would we say to a society that decided it was okay to leave the weak or disabled to die? Well, we might feel strongly that there are absolute values of right and wrong. But the naked truth is that without God, there is no objective morality.

Depressing, or just plain wrong?

I began this section by saying that I wasn't setting out to prove whether atheism (or 'naturalism') was right or wrong; I simply wanted to consider where it leads. If there is no God, what does it do to our view of the world, our longing for purpose, our desire for freedom, our quest for knowledge, and our sense of morality?

However, having thought through some of the consequences of naturalism, it's hard not to begin to doubt its validity.

One of the criteria we must use when we weigh up any belief system is whether it makes good sense of the world and how we experience it. The problem with naturalism (as we've been exploring it) is that it fails on this criterion. Naturalism just doesn't make sense of our experience of the world.

Imagine that you or a member of your family were the victim of a terrible personal crime. If you are going to live as a consistent naturalist, then you need to accept that there was nothing really wrong with what you experienced. Right and wrong are made-up values that only exist in our minds. Even if you are in terrible pain and grief, you can't appeal to any real objective measure that proves the perpetrator was wrong to do what they did. That is just how things are. Some people get hurt, and some people get lucky, but we're all just collections of atoms—just little parts of one, big meaningless cosmos.

How would you react to applying naturalism to a situation like this? One possible way is to try and live it out consistently: to accept that the criminal only acted the way he did because of his nature and nurture, and cannot be blamed; to accept that you are only hurt and angry about what has happened because of your own nature and nurture, and not because of any real, true standards of right and wrong; and to train yourself to appreciate that in a universe without a God we only think and feel the way we do about the ordeal because of the chemicals in our brains.

But is that really how you would react? Of course it's not. Nobody really lives like that. After such an experience, you are much more likely to reject naturalism as the truth. It fails to make sense of the world. We know that some things are right and other things are wrong. We know it in our personal experience, and we know it as we watch the news. How can we accept a view of the world that tells us *nothing* is objectively wrong?

And what about love? Naturalism makes a mockery of our feelings of love. I don't know if you've ever thought about why you love somebody. Perhaps there are things you love about them—their patience or their courage or the way they think about the world. Well, if naturalism were really true, our feelings of love for somebody would be utterly pointless. We only have them because it makes our genes more likely to survive. The qualities we love in the person we love are only there because they were caused by their own nature and environment. That person you love— it's just a complex machine. And as for your feelings of love for them, what are they other than chemical reactions in your own brain? You're just a machine too.

Again, when we consider the implications of naturalism here, it doesn't just come as a bit of bad news. It simply fails at a profound level to explain the world as we experience it. It doesn't make sense of our feelings. It doesn't make sense of the world around us. If an explanation of the universe fails to explain some of the key things we experience, then the best solution is not to stick with it and be depressed. The best solution is to look for the truth somewhere else.

CHAPTER 5

WHERE DO WE GO FROM HERE?

IN CHAPTER 1, I TOLD YOU ABOUT SIMON, THE GUY who didn't believe in God but didn't think it mattered either way. I hope that by now you've seen it really does matter.

We've done what many people never get round to doing—we've started with the assumption that there is no God, and followed it through to its logical conclusions. We've seen that if there is no God, there's no real meaning or purpose to our lives. We can choose to live for something, but we won't find any higher meaning or purpose for our lives, because we're just arrangements of atoms in a cosmos that doesn't care.

We've seen that the freedom we value is just an illusion, because we only do what our nature and our nurture compel us to do. We've seen that we can't trust our minds to lead us to the truth, so any conclusion we reach that God is not there is inherently unreliable.

We've seen that there is no real right and wrong—just things we like and things we don't like, based upon what we have decided to value the most. Other people and other societies have different values and different ideas about good and evil and human rights, but there is no right answer that we can appeal to outside of our human minds.

These truths are hard to hear. You might be thinking that, although you don't believe in God, this isn't the way you think about the world. But all we've done is think consistently about what it really means for there to be no God.

Where do we go from here? One option is to despair. Nothing is significant, nothing has any meaning, nothing can be known for certain, nothing we do is original or independent from our genetic programming, and nothing can be objectively judged as right or wrong. This outlook on the world is closely related to what's known as nihilism: the belief that our existence has no objective purpose, meaning or value.

But that's not a very attractive option. The alternative is simply to live in denial; to choose to ignore everything we've been thinking about. By choosing for ourselves a purpose, and living as though there actually is right and wrong and free will and knowledge, we can seek to live in a way that brings happiness and satisfaction. The universe might not contain any meaning, but we can think one up and at least live for that meaning ourselves.

But this, too, is terribly unattractive, because we would know deep down that we were living a lie. And we would know that even the very choice we make to embrace this sort of pretend life would have been determined by our genetic programming.

Although it might sound very strange to decide to live like this, in denial of the truth, it's actually what very many people do. James Sire puts it like this:

> Why, then, aren't most naturalists nihilists? The obvious answer is the best one: Most naturalists do not take their naturalism seriously. They are inconsistent. They affirm a set of values. They have friends who affirm a similar set. They appear to know and don't ask how they know they know. They seem to be able to choose and don't ask themselves whether their apparent freedom is really caprice or determinism. Socrates said that the unexamined life is not worth living, but for a naturalist he is wrong. For a naturalist it is the examined life that is not worth living.[15]

I think this is a very perceptive analysis. It certainly describes exactly what I would be most likely to do. If you talk about these issues with friends, then it's easy to agree that certain moral values are obvious. We might even say they are 'common sense'. And if they are so obvious, then maybe that's basically how everybody thinks. So we can carry on living by those values and just pretend that the uncomfortable truths we've seen so far aren't really out there.

This is what many people do today. They deny that there is a God, but they don't think about or live out the consequences. But we *are* thinking about the consequences. And once we've exposed the naked truth about life without God, it's impossible to pretend that our lives can still be built on meaning and morality and freedom and knowledge.

As well as being bleakly inconsistent, living in denial like this is also a seriously risky strategy. What if there is a God after all? And if there is a God, and we've decided to ignore that ultimate reality and choose our own meaning, then we're gambling on the possibility that our Creator won't mind about that. What if God does mind? What if it matters to him that we say there's probably no such thing as God but then live from day to day in a way that needs him to be there?

Yet from what we've seen so far, this is the choice we face. We can live in despair or we can live in denial. Will you be comfortable living like this?

There is another option. We can investigate whether or not God actually exists, because if he does, it would make all the difference in the world. For a start, it would mean that there really could be a purpose to our lives. There would be more to life than just living in a universe of "blind, pitiless indifference".

On 23 November 2003, my friend Debs had a horrific car accident. Debs crashed into a people carrier, and had to be cut out of her vehicle. Her liver had been lacerated and ruptured, she had serious internal bleeding, and she was left in a critical condition. When Debs regained consciousness several days later, she had no idea what had happened and she didn't know where she was.

Debs's parents are Christians, and when I visited her in hospital I was amazed by a sign they'd written for her by her bedside. It simply read, "Don't ask 'why?' Ask 'what for?' We believe all this will bring great glory to God and great blessing to many." Debs and her parents think that God does exist, and this clearly gives purpose and meaning to their lives, even in the face of tragedy.

If there was such a God, it would also make a difference to our freedom and knowledge. It would open up the possibility that we can make a difference to the world, instead of simply living and thinking according to our genetic programming.

If a God like this exists, there would also be objective morality. Our feelings that some things are right and other things are wrong would not just be subjective, made-up views. It would allow us to state with confidence that human beings matter and that they have rights, because they were created by a God who is concerned about evil and injustice.

This is what Martin Luther King Jr. knew when he stood at the Lincoln Memorial in Washington D.C. on 28 August 1963 and said, "I have a dream". Martin Luther King believed that the racial inequality and injustice he stood against was wrong. He didn't think it was just something he didn't like because of subjective ideas about morality. He believed it was wrong because he believed there is a God who had made all human beings equal. He made that clear throughout his magnificent speech, and the following section culminated in him quoting from the Bible:

> There are those who are asking the devotees of civil rights, "When will you be satisfied?" We can never be satisfied as long as the Negro is the victim of the unspeakable horrors of police brutality. We can never be satisfied as long as our bodies, heavy with the fatigue of travel, cannot gain lodging in the motels of the highways and the hotels of the cities. We cannot be satisfied as long as the Negro's basic mobility is from a smaller ghetto to a larger one. We can never be satisfied as long as our children are stripped of their self-hood and robbed of their dignity by signs stating: "For Whites Only". We cannot be satisfied as long as a Negro in Mississippi cannot vote and a Negro in New York believes he has nothing for which to vote. No, no, we are not satisfied, and we will not be satisfied until "justice rolls down like waters, and righteousness like a mighty stream".[16]

Purpose, freedom, knowledge and morality. In all of these areas, God would make all the difference. And our investigation so far has just been about while we're still alive. We also need to think about what happens when we die. If the God of Christianity exists, then all of us, when we die, face the prospect of living forever either with God or away from him. Obviously, this claim raises the stakes even further. And dramatically so.

A Christian called Dwight Moody, who knew he was sick and was going to die, was able to say, "Someday you will read in the papers that DL Moody of East Northfield is dead. Don't you believe a word of it! At that moment I shall be more alive than I am now."[17] Right now, reading that, you might think he was crazy. But we need to examine the evidence. Could DL Moody have been right? Is this possibility open to us as well?

With all this in mind, we know that God matters. We're ready to move on.

CHAPTER 6

NAKED GOD

I F YOU HAPPENED TO LOOK EVEN QUICKLY AT THE contents page, you will have noticed that there are lots of chapters in this book about Jesus. This is very deliberate. Instead of looking at arguments from science or philosophy, I primarily want to consider who Jesus was, and whether that changes our mind about God. It's not the approach everyone would take, so it merits an explanation.

One important reason is simply the weakness of other lines of enquiry. We could spend our lives reading the many scientific and philosophical books that argue for and against the existence of God, but there's a limit to how far they will take us. The problem is that science is not really able to tell us whether or not there is a God.

Imagine for a minute that advances in science genuinely meant that we could explain entirely in terms of natural causes how everything in the universe came into existence and continued to operate. Even then, could we be certain that God does not exist? What if there was still a God, but he had created an ordered universe, designed to function without the need for any actual or perceived supernatural intervention?

Dr Denis Alexander is a biochemist at Cambridge University, and in 2008 he released a book entitled *Creation and Evolution: Do we have to choose?* You can see already where he's going. He writes: "Those many Christians today who are active in the biological sciences are amazed as we uncover more and more of God's creative actions in our daily research. We do not look for God in the 'gaps' in our scientific knowledge, but instead worship God for the whole of his created order, including those remarkable evolutionary processes that God has used for his creative purposes."[18]

Dr Alexander's science is perfectly compatible with the idea of a creator God. For him, there is likely to be a God behind the ordered universe that scientists observe and investigate. In fact, the more we discover using science, the more Dr Alexander is impressed with that God.

Obviously if scientific advancement had proved there is no God, then we'd need to stop here. Having seen the naked truth about atheism, we'd be back with those options again—living in denial or in despair. But contrary to the way things are sometimes portrayed, science hasn't answered the God question.

This is important. I had a friend named Mark who started investigating Jesus. He said he found the evidence about Jesus very compelling, but then he stopped looking into it because he thought his background in biology would be incompatible with belief in God.

Other scientists, such as Richard Dawkins, would agree with Mark's view. Indeed, writers like Richard Dawkins have probably led Mark to think like that. We're now given the impression in the media that there's a war going on between those who believe in science and those who believe in God. But science and Christianity are not incompatible. In fact for many scientists, the sense of order we observe and discover in the universe points towards there having been an intelligent creator.

Dr Francis Collins, who until recently was head of the Human Genome Project, is a Christian who believes in evolutionary science. He was recorded in an interview summarizing his position, saying, "I'm a theistic evolutionist. I take the view that God, in his wisdom, used evolution as his creative scheme. I don't see why that's such a bad idea. That's pretty amazingly creative on his part. And what is wrong with that as a way of putting together in a synthetic way the view of God who is interested in creating a group of individuals that he can have fellowship with— us? Why is evolution not an appropriate way to get to that goal? I don't see a problem with that."[19]

It's not just Christians who have realized that science doesn't point us away from the existence of God. The late Stephen Jay Gould was an eminent scientist and an atheist. He wrote: "Either half my colleagues are enormously stupid, or else the science of Darwinism is fully compatible with conventional religious beliefs—and equally compatible with atheism."[20]

You might be somebody who doesn't accept that Darwinism explains everything anyway. But if you're somebody who does accept it, then it shouldn't preclude you from believing that the cosmos was created by a God. There might still be a God who used a process of evolution to create the great variety and complexity of life we have on earth today.

Science will give us lots of answers, but not to our questions about whether God exists. For these questions, we need a different line of enquiry.

But why Jesus? He's probably not somebody you talk about every day. At the start of this book, I reminded you of the surprising fuss caused in the early 1990s by the song, 'Let's talk about sex'. It's surprising now because, in the 21st century, people talk about sex all the time.

There are lots of things we'll now talk openly about. They used to say that you shouldn't mention sex, religion or politics, but those subjects are all on the agenda now. But the funny thing is that for all our openness, 'Jesus' seems to be a subject that is firmly out of bounds.

Have you noticed that? Of course people use the word—all the time. What I mean is that you're not supposed to mention Jesus the actual historical person.

If you don't believe me, just try it. Go on—give it a go. I've been trying it for a few years now, so I'm used to the reaction. If you're in a coffee shop with a friend, or you're on a night out, or you're meeting somebody new, just try asking them what they think about Jesus. I've seen some people physically shudder. Others have looked at me as if I've gone completely mad. Still others have given me a condescending smile.

The responses are so uniformly negative, I've even wondered whether you could use it as a tactic to get rid of unwelcome guests. Next time you've got a salesman at the door and he won't take no for an answer, try asking him about Jesus. The chances are, he'll run a mile and leave you in peace.

It's as if there's an unwritten rule that you don't mention Jesus in polite conversation. And this cultural taboo raises a couple of questions. One is: Why does his name feature so prominently in the chapters of this book? From a marketing point of view, it could be a disaster! But more fundamentally: Why is it that Jesus is so hard to talk about?

I think it's partly because we worry that anyone who starts talking about Jesus is trying to 'convert' us. Perhaps it also just seems too divisive. In a society where there are many different beliefs, we place a high priority on tolerance. Lots of people believe in a 'god' of some kind, but talking about Jesus might offend people. Or maybe we've just had bad experiences personally, either of church or with a Christian person. Maybe the word 'Jesus' makes us think of people in the street shouting at us with megaphones, and it all seems a bit radical.

There are plenty of reasons not to mention Jesus. But when you think about it, how many of them are actually about Jesus himself? Virtually everybody accepts that he was a real man who lived in the Middle East around 2000 years ago. Most people would go further and agree that he is one of the two or three most influential men who have ever lived. But we won't talk about him—not because of who he actually was, but because of what he has become in people's minds.

Everybody has a view about who Jesus was: a fine teacher, a dangerous revolutionary, a godly prophet, a deluded maniac, a miraculous healer, a devious trickster, God himself—the list goes on. We all have an opinion.

But the problem is that many of our opinions aren't based on good evidence. It's as if the real Jesus of the first century has been covered up. We've picked up various ideas about him from school, from friends, from the media, from parents, from churches, and from just about anywhere he's mentioned. Sometimes people have been honestly mistaken, sometimes they've been reckless about the truth, and sometimes they've flat out lied. But from my observation, and from (awkward) conversations with many friends, most people have a jumbled and confused view of Jesus based on a mix of true, half-true and false ideas. And then, in general conversation, we hardly talk about him.

We need to go back to the evidence and uncover the truth about Jesus. Who was this man? Why did he attract such a following? Why do so many people today say they follow him? What does the reliable evidence about him reveal?

When we investigate Jesus, we'll fairly quickly discover that he was a man who claimed he was God. This might not sound particularly surprising, but it actually singles Jesus out. When Jesus claimed to be God, he did something that no other founder of a major world religion has ever done. Other religions were founded by people who claimed to be prophets, or to have special teaching from God or special access to God. But those founders did not claim to *be* God. Among the major religious leaders of the world, only Jesus did that.

Now, that's not enough in itself. There are lots of people over history who have claimed to be God. Most of them were quickly written off as being deluded, and some of them attracted cult followings briefly in their own time.

But with Jesus, it's different. When Jesus claimed to be God, people believed him. Lots of people. His followers claimed that he performed the kind of miraculous works God would do, that he taught as nobody had ever taught before, and that he was a man of extraordinary character. They even claimed that after he died, he came back to life again. These are things we can investigate.

If we were going to look through history and find all of the people who have ever claimed to be God-in-the-flesh, we'd find that one of those people stands dramatically apart from the rest. Jesus didn't just make this extraordinary claim. He has persuaded countless millions down through the centuries to believe it, and to devote their lives to his service. In the West, we still mark our calendars according to when he was born. And many of the values and beliefs we take for granted in Western civilization spring from his teaching.

This shows us why Jesus is worth investigating. At some stage we've got to look closely for ourselves and work out once and for all whether Jesus was right when he made these claims. If we decide he was wrong, what have we lost? Surely it would still have been worth our time examining the evidence about a man who claimed so much and has influenced so many.

Alternatively, we might decide he was right. If we decide he was telling the truth, then he shows us that God exists. And it goes further than that, because he also shows us how to relate to God. We don't just end up with an abstract idea that there seems to be an intelligent creator of the universe. We find a God who is personal, and interested in knowing us. Jesus could be the answer we're looking for, because he claimed to be God as a man, God in the flesh, God exposed. Jesus claimed to be Naked God.

Having seen the naked truth about life without God, we know how much this matters. The purpose of this book is to uncover the truth about God, and the way to do that is to do the same for Jesus. He made extraordinary claims about himself, and we need to find out whether he was right. We need to look at the evidence and work out who the real Jesus actually was. Our culture has dressed him up in all sorts of ways, and we've formed opinions about him, often based on false evidence and hearsay. We need to strip away those false ideas and uncover the real Jesus—the historical Jesus. We need to move on from the naked truth to the naked Jesus.

PART II

NAKED JESUS

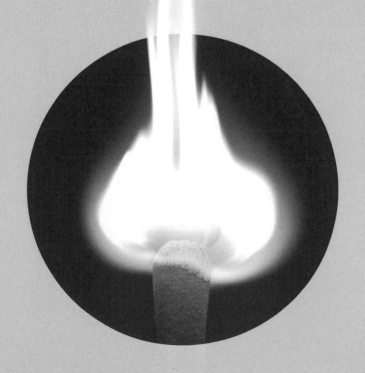

CHAPTER 7

CLEARING THE GROUND

As we set off on our next stage, we must deal with two major objections. These objections are widely held all around us, and are assumed to be true by many intelligent, thoughtful people. I used to feel these objections quite strongly towards the claims of Jesus. They are objections so serious that if they were true, they would be enough to bring an end to our investigation.

Objection: Isn't Jesus just one of many valid options?

My friend Andy asked me about Christianity one day, and he said to me, "What Christians do, which I would never do, is they say that their religion is right and other religions are wrong. It's arrogant to say that."

The position Andy articulated is known as relativism. It's the view that all beliefs about God are equally valid. It's an important objection, because it stands squarely in the face of Jesus' claims to be the one true God. If Jesus really did reveal the whole truth about God, it would mean that other religions are wrong when they contradict what we find out from Jesus.

Relativism is very popular. Have you ever heard anybody say, "Whatever you choose to believe is true for you"? Do you yourself think that different religions are all equally valid, and that people shouldn't try to persuade each other that their particular faith is best? This is what I was taught in assemblies at school.

A common illustration used by relativists is of a mountain with different paths all leading to the top. People are walking up the different paths, but they can't see the paths on the other sides of the mountain. In this analogy, God, or the truth about him, is at the top of the mountain. The different paths are the different religions leading up to God.

If this is correct, then when we look at a religion we shouldn't be asking, "Is it true?" Instead we should ask, "Does it work for me?" Is this the path up the mountain that will suit me best? If so, then that's the faith for me. You have your path and I have mine. If I'm okay, and you are okay, then everyone is okay.

Relativism sounds very attractive. The world is crying

CLEARING THE GROUND · 61

out for more tolerance of other people's beliefs. If all religions are equally valid, then people of different faiths can live side-by-side in harmony. You might have taken a relativist position about the different beliefs of people you know. If some of your friends are Muslims, and others are Jewish, and others atheists, it can seem loving and tolerant to say, "I'm glad you have your faith and it works for you. As long as you find it personally fulfilling, that is what counts."

But things aren't so simple. Yes, people believe different things about God. But we have different reasons for believing what we do, and not all of them are good or solid reasons. We might believe some things because of the influence of our parents, friends, society and culture, but what if those influences have got it wrong? We might believe things because they provide us with psychological comfort, or peace of mind or independence, but again this might lead us to believe something that is simply not true.

Relativism doesn't evaluate the reasons for believing something. It doesn't treat our questions about God as issues of truth. Instead, it treats them as issues of taste or opinion.

Choosing a football team to support is an issue of taste. It's a preference or opinion—there isn't a right or wrong. I grew up supporting my local team, which is Middlesbrough, and I liked them because they were the club for my home town. In my childhood excitement, I never thought to check whether this was a club that would actually win games and bring me happiness. I was too young to heed the warnings of the fan who has written a book about supporting Middlesbrough entitled *The first 35 years are the worst*.

Other people choose to support a team that wins all the time, or plays attractive football. When you support a club like Middlesbrough, which has won one trophy in the past 130 years, such people are hard to live with. But the truth is that there's no rule against it, and I've got no right to be annoyed. There's no right or wrong in choosing your favourite football team. It's an issue of taste, family background and personal circumstances.

Issues of truth are different. While the issue of which football team we support is one of taste, the issue of which football team won the FA Cup final in 1988 is a question of truth. Regardless of which football team we support, and no matter what we choose to believe, Wimbledon famously won the FA Cup that year.

This is the fundamental problem with relativism. The question of whether God exists or not is an issue of truth, not taste. Either there is no God, or there is one God or there are many gods, and the truth (or otherwise) of these statements doesn't depend on our own preferences or opinions. That somebody believes something about God does not make it true—or false. God either exists, or he does not exist. He is either interested in us, or he is not. If God is real, the whole world could deny that fact, and yet it would still be true.

This is also important when we begin to consider who Jesus is. Either Jesus died and came back to life again, as his early followers claim, or something different happened.

This is a claim about an historical event, and it's crucial to our investigation. We need to look at these issues of truth, and decide what makes best sense of all the evidence.

This is where relativism starts to break down. It insists that all religions are equally valid, and that none of them are 'true' or 'false', 'right' or 'wrong'. But the various major world religions make vastly different assertions about who Jesus was and what happened in history.

Christians believe that Jesus was God's anointed one (or Christ), that he was killed by crucifixion, and that he came back to life as the ruler of the world. Modern Judaism insists that Jesus was not God's anointed one, that he most definitely did not come to back to life again, and that Israel is still waiting for a Christ to come. Islam claims that Jesus was a prophet, but emphatically denies that he was ever crucified or rose from the dead. Buddhism claims that there isn't even a personal God in the first place, let alone that Jesus could have been sent by such a God into the world.

Clearly, there are crucial contradictions between these religions. But relativism says that if you choose one of those sets of claims then it's true for you. In what sense could this possibly be valid logically or rationally? If Islam is true for a Muslim, who says that Jesus was not God and did not die on a cross, how could Christianity also be true for a Christian who fervently believes the opposite? Either Jesus died by crucifixion or he didn't; either he was divine or he was not. Different faiths make real, contradictory and critically important historical claims.

We are left asking how relativism can be a valid or rational response to reality. In fact, although it may sound strange at first, we are also left with the conclusion that relativism is itself a rather arrogant way of thinking.

Relativism claims that it is arrogant to think any one set of religious claims is really 'true'. But for this relativistic statement to be true, all of the distinctive features of the major world religions have to be stripped away or declared false. It is only a drastically edited Islam and a drastically edited Christianity that can be said to be basically teaching the same thing.

The relativist ends up saying that he knows better than the actual adherents of the different religions. Actual Christians and actual Muslims know very well that their religious truth claims are poles apart, and contain irreconcilable contradictions. They can continue to respect each other despite these differences, but they don't pretend the differences aren't there. However, the relativist declares that he or she really knows that the two religions are basically teaching the same thing, and heading in the same direction with the same aims and goals.

The relativist objects to anybody who says their faith is more valid than anybody else's. But what's really going on is that the relativist is imposing his or her own particular view of God upon everyone else—the view that God, if he exists, doesn't mind what we believe or do. Relativism does exactly what it says no other person is allowed to do: it 'absolutizes' its view of truth and religion and God.

If we go back to the picture of the different paths up the same mountain, it's worth thinking about where the relativist is standing in the picture. The relativist needs to be in a helicopter above the mountain! The religious people in the world can't see that there are other paths leading up the same mountain to the same summit. Only the relativist from his superior vantage point can see all of the paths at once, and see where they lead. It needn't be that way. The 'paths' of different religious people could be leading up entirely different mountains, or some of the paths could be leading to dead ends. But the relativist knows best.

You can understand why relativism is popular and is taught in schools. We all want there to be tolerance between different religions. It seems quite wrong that people should be discriminated against simply for what they believe.

But this is where Christianity provides an immensely better solution. There is a world of difference between saying that what somebody believes is not right, and saying that they have no right to believe it. Although some ideologies might justify intolerance, one of the most famous things Jesus taught was that we should love our enemies. He challenged people not just to love and tolerate those who disagree with them, but to love even those who hate them and wish them harm. Following the teaching of Jesus would lead us to abhor racism, bigotry and religious intolerance.

This is the real answer. Jesus promoted tolerance, but he did it differently. Relativism does it by attempting not to draw lines. Against all rational thought, it says that contradictory truth claims are equally valid. On the other hand, Jesus did draw lines. He made statements about himself and God that are matters of truth, not taste. He drew lines, but he promoted tolerance by teaching us how we should treat people who are on the other side of the line to us. He taught us to love those who completely disagree with us, and even those who hate us.

If we were to put Jesus' teaching into practice, we would be tolerant of people who have different positions of faith to our own. But for the reasons we have considered, this tolerance should not lead us to accept that every belief about God is as valid and true as any other. Jesus is not just one of a number of valid options. If his claims to be God are true, then they are true regardless of what people believe. We need to investigate him and consider for ourselves what makes best sense of the evidence.

Objection: Isn't Jesus just a made-up legend?

It's fairly common these days to hear sweeping statements made about the almost fictional nature of the New Testament. "It was all written long after Jesus … We all know that it was changed and modified and that there have been lots of errors in copying and translation … The Apostle Paul really invented Christianity and made Jesus into a 'god' … And the church has probably doctored the Bible as well in order to maintain its power …" And so on. Think of Dan Brown's *The Da Vinci Code* and Philip Pullman's book *The Good Man Jesus and the Scoundrel Christ*.

This second objection would also bring our investigation of Jesus crashing to a halt. Our plan is to assess the claims Jesus made about himself, but before we do that we need to know whether he actually made them.

When I worked as a lawyer, I used to handle my fair share of witness statements. Some were more reliable than others. I worked on one trial where the judge said that trying to work out how the witness statements had been put together was like trying to understand what was going on in the front row of a rugby scrum. He was suspicious that the different witness statements had been written in a mysterious, collaborative way, and it cast doubt on the testimony of the witnesses.

And yet reliable witness evidence is often what wins a case. People can always speculate about events, and construct elaborate theories, but there's no substitute for hearing what actually happened from the people who were actually there. For a few years, I worked on a case defending the Bank of England. The claim rested on a conspiracy theory that accused some of the leading Bank of England staff of dishonesty in the way they had supervised a bank. A lot of these allegations were made by a brilliant barrister in an opening speech that went on for a staggering and exhausting 86 days. The newspapers were printing what was being said in court, and a detailed theory was put together of how the Bank of England supervisors had conspired together.

But after all of that argument, put forward persuasively and eloquently at great, great length, the claim collapsed when the witnesses got into the box. Once the witness evidence was considered, the conspiracy theory fell apart. The lengthy and brilliant speculation about what had happened was dismissed in favour of the testimonies of the men and women who had actually been there at the time, and who could report back what had really happened.

Do we have this kind of vital eyewitness testimony about Jesus? Many people today take the view that we do not—that the documents about Jesus are unreliable, that they were written a long time after the events they describe, that the claims they contain have been embellished and exaggerated, and that the manuscripts have been tampered with and corrupted over the centuries. Dan Brown's *The Da Vinci Code* did much to spread and popularize this view in recent times.

What should we make of this objection?

Who wrote the books?

We can start by noting that the four biographies (or 'Gospels') of Jesus' life that we find in the Bible all claim to be based on eyewitness evidence. They are each named after their authors: Matthew, Mark, Luke and John. Matthew and John were two of Jesus' 12 closest followers or disciples. Mark was a close associate of Peter, another of Jesus' disciples.[21] And Luke knew the eyewitnesses, who were the key leaders in the early church. He begins his Gospel by explaining, "Therefore, since I myself have carefully investigated everything from the beginning, it seemed good also to me to write an orderly account for you, most excellent Theophilus".[22]

As you read the Gospels, it is abundantly clear that the biographers themselves don't think they are writing about a legend, nor do the documents read like legends or myths. The Gospels read like eyewitness reports. They contain specific details that don't seem to be particularly relevant and that only eyewitnesses would be able to recall. At one point Mark writes that Jesus was asleep on a cushion;[23] at another point, John records that Peter and his friends caught 153 fish.[24]

The writers clearly wanted their books to be read as historically accurate biographies. For example, when Luke writes about John the Baptist, he begins by telling us that John started his work "in the fifteenth year of the reign of Tiberius Caesar—when Pontius Pilate was governor of Judea, Herod tetrarch of Galilee, his brother Philip tetrarch of Iturea and Traconitis, and Lysanias tetrarch of Abilene —during the high priesthood of Annas and Caiaphas ..."[25] Luke wants his readers to know that these events took place at a particular time in history.

You sometimes hear people say that the New Testament was written long after Jesus was alive, but this is simply not what the experts know to be true. There is a wide consensus among both Christian and non-Christian scholars that these documents were all written within the lifetimes of the eyewitnesses.[26] At the time the Gospels were written, the people who had been there to see Jesus and know him were still alive, and they could easily have refuted any wild or exaggerated claims. You cannot create a legend while eyewitnesses are still around. If any of these accounts was a fabrication, it would have easily been discredited at the time.

All of this is good news. Many of our concerns are alleviated simply by learning who wrote the Gospels and when they were written. The Gospel authors weren't powerful religious leaders or conspirators. They were very ordinary men who knew Jesus and who suffered terribly for their testimonies about him.

Are we reading what they wrote?

Between us and those original biographies of Jesus stands a long span of time—now nearly two millennia. It has led some to suspect that the Gospels must surely have become corrupted from their original form. But here again, the evidence is overwhelming that what we have in our possession today are authentic copies of those original documents.

In order to appreciate how strong the evidence for the New Testament is, it's worth realizing what manuscript support exists for other important ancient historical documents. For example, Caesar's *The Gallic Wars* was written around 50 BC, but the oldest surviving copy is from 825 AD. As well as this gap of 875 years, we only have ten ancient copies of the document in existence today. Tacitus' *Histories and Annals* is the chief source of information we have about the Roman world in New

Testament times. It was written around 100 AD, but the oldest surviving copy is from 850 AD and only two ancient copies survive.[27]

By contrast, the New Testament was written between roughly 50 and 90 AD, the earliest copy of part of it dates from 120 AD, and we still have over 5,000 ancient manuscripts of all or part of the New Testament in Greek, its original language. Most of the New Testament, including all four Gospels, is preserved in a manuscript from 250 AD, and we have a complete copy of the entire New Testament from 350 AD.[28] In addition to the manuscript copies we have in the original Greek language, the New Testament was translated from an early date, and we have over 18,000 manuscripts in other languages. And even if we didn't have any of these thousands of ancient manuscripts and translations, virtually the entire New Testament could also be reconstructed from quotations contained in letters, treatises and books written by Christians within 250 years of its composition.

We're looking at two factors here that give us considerable confidence that the New Testament we have today is accurate: the number of ancient copies in existence, and the proximity in time between those copies and the original documents. On both counts, the evidence for the New Testament is outstanding, and far outweighs any other document of antiquity.

Sir Frederic Kenyon was the director and principal librarian of the British Museum, and an expert on ancient texts and their authority. He wrote the following summary of the confidence we can have in our copies of the New Testament:

> The interval then between the dates of the original composition (of the New Testament) and the earliest extant evidence becomes so small as to be in fact negligible, and the last foundation for any doubt that the Scriptures have come down to us substantially as they were written has now been removed. Both the *authenticity* and the *general integrity* of the books of the New Testament may be regarded as finally established.[29]

Finally, what we know about Jesus from other historical sources also supports the claims of the Gospels. For example, from the Jewish historian Josephus and the Roman historian Tacitus, we know that Jesus attracted a large following and that he was crucified under Pontius Pilate following allegations by the Jewish leaders.[30]

You might be finding all of this evidence surprising. It seems almost commonly accepted today that the New Testament documents must have been written or re-written several hundred years after Jesus lived. But it is remarkable how badly this common view fits with the facts. The Gospels were written far too early to be legends, and we have more than enough early copies of them to show with confidence that they didn't become corrupted.

I realize that if you've heard before that the New Testament is inaccurate, it can be quite a change to accept it as history. But the evidence points very strongly in this direction. (If you would like to chase this evidence further, and read about these issues in more detail, see the 'Further Reading' listed in the appendix on page 185.)

No matter what we have heard or thought or read in a Dan Brown novel, we must change our view in light of the overwhelming evidence that the New Testament contains reliable historical documents written using eyewitness testimony. Now we must turn to those documents and investigate Jesus for ourselves.

CHAPTER 8

ISN'T JESUS JUST A GOOD MORAL TEACHER?

In considering the naked truth of life without God, we came to understand how important it is to investigate the real Jesus. We have established that he cannot simply be dismissed either as one of many options or as a legend. The next step is to turn to the first-century documents and ask the ultimate question: "Who is Jesus?"

His identity certainly captured the imagination of the people who met him in the first century. When his followers were with him in a dangerous storm on the Sea of Galilee, Jesus spoke to the wind and the waves, and they became completely calm. His disciples were terrified, and asked each other, "Who is this? Even the wind and the waves obey him!"[31] When Jesus said to a man, "Friend, your sins are forgiven", the religious leaders asked, "Who is this fellow who speaks blasphemy? Who can forgive sins but God alone?"[32] Herod Antipas, who ruled over the regions of Galilee and Perea for the Romans, heard about Jesus and asked, "Who, then, is this I hear such things about?"[33]

It's very common to think that Jesus was a good moral teacher but nothing more. In *The Penguin Book of Historic Speeches*, editor Brian Macarthur writes: "nearly 2,000 years later, the moral code contained in the Sermon on the Mount remains the foundation of Western morality".[34] In fact, this is how Jesus is remembered by many people and even in many churches today. Although he might not be thought of as divine, or capable of miracles, his teaching is still regarded as relevant and even awe-inspiring.

It certainly seems right to remember that Jesus was the source of some outstanding moral teaching. Many people at the time of Jesus agreed that he taught in a new way and with new authority.[35] He told his followers how to live, advocating a life of love, forgiveness, service and sacrifice. But Jesus didn't just teach people how they should treat each other. A large proportion of Jesus' teaching was actually about himself. We cannot separate these elements in his teaching—they are bound together. As we investigate the real Jesus, we must turn to consider all of what he taught, including the claims he made about his own identity and mission.

His claims

Jesus was the son of a carpenter, brought up in the small town of Nazareth in the north of modern-day Israel. But right from the start of his ministry, he made astonishing claims about himself.

For example, Jesus began his teaching in the Jewish synagogues, and one Saturday he returned to the synagogue of his home town. That day the chosen reading was from a prophet called Isaiah, who lived and wrote in the 7th century BC. As was customary, Jesus stood up to read from Isaiah. What happened next, though, was anything but customary. After Jesus was handed the scroll, Luke records what happened:

Unrolling it, he found the place where it is written:

"The Spirit of the Lord is on me,
    because he has anointed me
    to preach good news to the poor.
He has sent me to proclaim freedom for the
        prisoners
    and recovery of sight for the blind,
to release the oppressed,
    to proclaim the year of the Lord's favour."

Then he rolled up the scroll, gave it back to the attendant and sat down. The eyes of everyone in the synagogue were fastened on him, and he began by saying to them, "Today this scripture is fulfilled in your hearing."[36]

Jesus made the extraordinary claim that he was the fulfilment of Old Testament Scripture. He claimed to be God's
anointed one (or 'Christ') whom the Jewish people had
been waiting for. He made this claim at the start of his
ministry, and repeated it consistently. Later, when some
Jews wanted to kill him because of these claims, he was
bold enough to say, "You diligently study the Scriptures
because you think that by them you possess eternal life.
These are the Scriptures that testify about me, yet you
refuse to come to me to have life."[37]

There are other aspects to Jesus' shocking teaching about
himself. He taught that he had a unique relationship with the
Creator, whom he referred to as his Father. At a Jewish
festival in Jerusalem known as the Feast of Dedication, Jesus
said, "I and the Father are one". The Jews fully understood
the seriousness of this statement, and some even wanted to
stone Jesus. But Jesus said to them, "I have shown you many
great miracles from the Father. For which of these do
you stone me?" "We are not stoning you for any of these,"
replied the Jews, "but for blasphemy, because you, a mere
man, claim to be God".[38]

Jesus also claimed to have a unique authority to solve
the world's problems. He said, "Come to me, all you who
are weary and burdened, and I will give you rest".[39] On
another occasion he said, "I am the light of the world.
Whoever follows me will never walk in darkness, but will
have the light of life."[40] What sort of person thinks he is
the answer to everyone's questions?

He even claimed to have the authority to judge people.[41]

Twice in the biographies, Jesus told someone that "Your sins are forgiven". It's a bizarre claim unless you think you are God. Imagine that you did me some wrong, and then somebody else (whom neither of us knew) came along and said they were prepared to forgive you for it. What would be the sense in that? I am the one who has been hurt. What right does anybody else have to forgive you? Jesus was teaching that he had the right to judge and to forgive because he had divine authority over all people.

During the early period of Jesus' ministry, news about him spread far and wide. When the time came for a great Jewish festival known as the Feast of Tabernacles, many Jews travelled to Jerusalem in order to celebrate together. Amid growing excitement and expectation, Jesus arrived in Jerusalem halfway through the feast and began to teach people in the courts of the temple. John then records: "On the last and greatest day of the Feast, Jesus stood and said in a loud voice, 'If anyone is thirsty, let him come to me and drink. Whoever believes in me, as the Scripture has said, streams of living water will flow from within him.'"[42]

Mad, bad or God?

What are we to conclude from what Jesus taught about himself? The real Jesus clearly wasn't a meek and mild teacher of morality. He claimed to be the promised Christ of God, to be the unique Son of God, and to have authority over the world. These claims are simply astonishing. Nobody who is simply a good moral teacher could get away with such self-promotion. Either these claims were true and Jesus was God, or he was deluded, or he was a liar. Having considered Jesus' claims, the writer CS Lewis summed up our options as follows:

> I am trying here to prevent anyone saying the really foolish thing that people often say about him: "I'm ready to accept Jesus as a great moral teacher, but I don't accept his claim to be God." That is the one thing we must not say. A man who was merely a man and said the sort of things Jesus said would not be a great moral teacher. He would either be a lunatic—on a level with the man who says he is a poached egg—or else he would be the Devil of Hell. You must make your choice. Either this man was, and is, the Son of God: or else a madman or something worse. You can shut him up for a fool, you can spit at him and kill him as a demon; or you can fall at his feet and call him Lord and God. But let us not come with any patronising nonsense about his being a great human teacher. He has not left that open to us. He did not intend to.[43]

The magnitude of Jesus' claims leaves us with these options, and this will be important to remember as we consider other evidence about who he was. However, it's worth pausing and considering Richard Dawkins's recent challenge to CS Lewis's 'trilemma'. In *The God Delusion* Dawkins writes:

> A common argument ... states that since Jesus
> claimed to be the Son of God, he must have been
> either right or else insane or a liar: 'Mad, Bad or
> God' ... The historical evidence that Jesus claimed
> any sort of divine status is minimal. But even if the
> evidence were good, the trilemma on offer would
> be ludicrously inadequate. A fourth possibility,
> almost too obvious to need mentioning, is that
> Jesus was honestly mistaken.[44]

Dawkins raises two objections, the first being that there is
a lack of historical evidence that Jesus claimed divine
status. As we've already seen, even in a brief survey of
some of Jesus' claims about himself, there is more than
enough evidence that Jesus considered himself to be God's
Son (and we haven't considered the many other examples
in the Gospels that make the same point).

Dawkins' second objection is that there is another possibility apart from the three offered by CS Lewis, namely
that Jesus was "honestly mistaken". But this is exactly what
CS Lewis meant by the possibility that Jesus was mad. A
man who honestly and sincerely believes himself to be the
Son of God—when he is nothing of the kind—is deluded.
We would normally suggest he visit a psychiatrist. Dawkins
hasn't raised a fourth category at all—he has simply taken
one of the three possibilities CS Lewis outlined and given
it a slightly different name.

Lewis's three options are the only three that can make
sense of a man who teaches the things that Jesus taught

about himself. Was he mad? Was he a deliberate liar? If these options do not fit the facts, then no matter how improbable it may seem to us, the only remaining possibility is that he was who he claimed to be. With this framework in mind, in the next chapter we will consider several strands of evidence, beginning with Jesus' character.

CHAPTER 9

WHO IS JESUS?

1. His character

The movie *Good Will Hunting* tells the story of Will Hunting, a young, troubled genius who is helped by psychologist Sean Maguire. After an arrogant outburst one day from Will, Sean challenges him with the fact that, despite all his intellectual ability, there is much he has never experienced. Sean begins by saying, "You've never been out of Boston. So if I asked you about art, you'd probably give me the skinny on every art book ever written. Michelangelo, you know a lot about him—life's work, political aspirations, him and the Pope, sexual orientation, the whole works, right? But I'll bet you can't tell me what it smells like in the Sistine Chapel. You've never actually stood there and looked up at that beautiful ceiling; seen that."[45]

I was reminded of that moment in the movie when I came to prepare this chapter, because the same could be said about the character of Jesus. There is a world of difference between knowing the facts about something and actually experiencing it for yourself. I could quote any number of people—past or present—who would describe Jesus with great rhetoric and praise. Napoleon, for example, wrote: "Everything in Christ astonishes me. His spirit overawes me, and his will confounds me. Between him and whoever else in the world, there is no possible term of comparison. He is truly a being by himself. … I search in vain in history to find the similar to Jesus Christ, or anything which can approach the gospel. Neither history, nor humanity, nor the ages, nor nature, offer me anything with which I am able to compare it or to explain it. Here everything is extraordinary."[46]

Yet in order to appreciate the character of Jesus ourselves, we need to try and experience it in some way for ourselves. There is no substitute for putting ourselves in the shoes of the men and women who were there in the first century with him, and imagining what it would have been like to have somebody like this among us. In this chapter, that's what we'll try to do.

Shortly after Jesus had shocked the synagogue in Nazareth with his claim to fulfil the Old Testament prophecy, he chose and called his first disciples, the men who were to become his closest followers throughout his life. They were fishermen. They were not kings or governors or respectable officials. Jesus claimed to be the

Son of God and the ruler of the world, but he spent most of his time with ordinary men and women. A modern equivalent would be Jesus making a speech claiming to be the One the world was waiting for, and then going into the local supermarket and asking the men and women at the checkout desks to come and be his closest followers for life. The only special thing about these men was their ordinariness.[47]

Jesus went on to spend his life with the outsiders of society. He ate with tax collectors, who were ostracized in their community as corrupt swindlers.[48] He always had time for the poor and the marginalized. He was a man of great humility and without pretensions, a character trait that's particularly surprising given his astonishingly grandiose claims.

People sometimes say you can tell a man by the company he keeps. What they mean is that it's a bad sign to find somebody spending a lot of time with disreputable people. Among the religious people of Jesus' time, this was taken to its extreme. The Jewish leaders believed they could remain clean and pure if they kept away from certain kinds of people. They were careful not to let other people drag them down.

Jesus stood out as a radical contrast to this prevailing attitude. The religious elite grumbled that he spent his time with people of ill repute. But he did it out of love and compassion. According to Jesus, it wasn't the food you ate or the company you kept that made you a bad person.

Another testimony to the character of Jesus was the

way people flocked to him when they needed help. Mark gives us two examples that occurred on the same day as Jesus arrived in a new town by the Sea of Galilee, involving two people from very different ends of society.

> When Jesus had again crossed over by boat to the other side of the lake, a large crowd gathered around him while he was by the lake. Then one of the synagogue rulers, named Jairus, came there. Seeing Jesus, he fell at his feet and pleaded earnestly with him, "My little daughter is dying. Please come and put your hands on her so that she will be healed and live." So Jesus went with him.[49]

We are not told much about Jairus, but we are told enough to know that he was a respectable man. He was a synagogue ruler, a job of considerable prestige in the community. It takes a lot for a family man with a respectable job to fall at somebody's feet. Yet when he heard that Jesus had arrived, and knowing his compassion and power, Jairus sought him out for help. His daughter was dying. He had nowhere else to turn.

Jesus had arrived in the town to find a large crowd of people. His popularity was obvious, and he could have spent his time with any number of people. His priority was teaching the crowds.[50] Yet when Jairus came to Jesus, Mark tells us that Jesus went with him.

When Jesus set out with Jairus, this must have caused some disappointment in the crowd. Other people wanted to be with Jesus, some of them with great needs of their own. Mark writes about one such woman, and in just a few words we are introduced to what must have been a life of great suffering.

> A large crowd followed and pressed around him. And a woman was there who had been subject to bleeding for twelve years. She had suffered a great deal under the care of many doctors and had spent all she had, yet instead of getting better she grew worse. When she heard about Jesus, she came up behind him in the crowd and touched his cloak, because she thought, "If I just touch his clothes, I will be healed." Immediately her bleeding stopped and she felt in her body that she was freed from her suffering.
>
> At once Jesus realized that power had gone out from him. He turned around in the crowd and asked, "Who touched my clothes?"
>
> "You see the people crowding against you," his disciples answered, "and yet you can ask, 'Who touched me?'"
>
> But Jesus kept looking around to see who had done it. Then the woman, knowing what had happened to her, came and fell at his feet and, trembling with fear, told him the whole truth. He said to her, "Daughter, your faith has healed you. Go in peace and be freed from your suffering."[51]

Mark records that the woman was miraculously healed, and you might find this hard to accept. For the moment, we are interested in Jesus' character and not his miracles. You might think it's weird that people believe in miracles, but we are going to address that issue shortly. For now, let's focus on the sort of person Jesus was.

Jesus could have just continued on, but he stopped and turned to find the woman. He heard her story, and comforted her even though she was afraid of him. His last words to her—"Go in peace and be freed from your suffering"—encapsulate the compassion that had drawn her to him.

From a respectable man in high society, to a sick woman who had nothing left, Jesus wanted to help. These are just two examples of a pattern in his ministry. Jesus was frequently moved with compassion towards the hungry, the bereaved, the blind and the sick. Conventional barriers were broken down. He sacrificed his reputation out of love for the desperate and the downcast.[52]

Moving on to the end of Jesus' life, and the night he was betrayed and arrested, John records the following example of Jesus' character:

> Jesus knew that the Father had put all things under his power, and that he had come from God and was returning to God; so he got up from the meal, took off his outer clothing, and wrapped a towel around his waist. After that, he poured water into a basin and began to wash his disciples' feet, drying them with the towel that was wrapped around him.[53]

In the ancient world, washing feet was one of the most

demeaning jobs for a slave. And the feet of the disciples would have been covered in dirt from the dry, dusty roads. They looked up to Jesus as their teacher and guide. They had heard him make his audacious claims, and they had watched him teach men, women and children in their thousands. But he didn't lord it over anyone. His extraordinary character was displayed that evening as he washed their smelly dirty feet in a basin, and dried them with the towel he had wrapped around his waist.

Later that night, Jesus was betrayed by one of his disciples, and arrested. The following day he was handed over to the Roman authorities to be executed by crucifixion. Even then, Jesus showed his love for mankind:

> When they came to the place called the Skull,
> there they crucified him, along with the
> criminals—one on his right, the other on his left.
> Jesus said, "Father, forgive them, for they do not
> know what they are doing."[54]

By this time, he had been rejected by the people, betrayed by one of his followers, arrested by the religious leaders, denied by a friend, abandoned by his disciples, flogged, mocked and nailed to a cross. Yet he was moved to pray for those who were responsible, asking his Father to forgive them.

These are just a few examples that demonstrate what Jesus was like. Throughout the Gospels, we encounter a man of extraordinary humility, love and compassion. His character captivated many people during his life, and has moved, changed and inspired countless others since.

As we consider these first-century accounts of Jesus' life, a startling paradox emerges. We find a man who made audacious claims about himself, but also a man with an astonishing character. The man who said, "All authority in heaven and on earth has been given to me", lived a life of unparalleled humility and love.[55] There truly has never been anybody like him. We can find people in history who have made very bold claims, and we can find people in history who have lived lives of incredible compassion and humility. But never in the history of humanity has there been such a combination of the two—a man with such an extraordinary character who has made such extraordinary claims.

Remembering the three possibilities (Lord, liar or lunatic), we have to weigh up these indications of Jesus' character, and ask ourselves whether he strikes us as either a liar or a madman. It is hard to find words suitable to describe Jesus' character: his balance, his humility, his compassion, his love. He was excellent, not in the overused sense of the word today, but in the sense that he was superior to everyone else. He was amazing, again not in the way we use the word today to describe everything that is vaguely good, but in the real sense that he overwhelms us with wonder. He lived a life without precedent, a beautiful life. For my money, it is inconceivable that this person could have been a deceiver or a fool.

If we had never heard of Jesus, we could never have conceived of somebody like this. And yet when we encounter him in the books of the New Testament, isn't he just what we would expect? If the universe does have a creator and he did come into the world at this one point in history, he would be bound to make the sort of claims that Jesus made. And yet, unlike other men and women who make outrageous claims, we would expect God—the creator of the whole universe—to live a life of complete consistency. As we examine the exemplary character of this Nazarene carpenter, we glimpse something beyond humanity. We see a unique personality that is perfectly in accord with his claim to be the Son of God.

Having examined this strand of evidence, we move on to consider Jesus' teaching.

2. His teaching

We have already seen that it is very difficult to regard Jesus as a great human teacher and nothing more. All the same, he is remembered as a great teacher for a reason. When Jesus taught the crowds, he spoke words that moved humanity forward. We will look at several examples as we consider who Jesus was.

Luke records a talk Jesus once gave to a massive crowd. Luke writes: "He went down with them and stood on a level place. A large crowd of his disciples was there and a great number of people from all over Judea, from Jerusalem, and from the coast of Tyre and Sidon, who had come to hear him and to be healed of their diseases."[56]

Part way through the talk, Jesus taught them this:

"But I tell you who hear me: Love your enemies, do good to those who hate you, bless those who curse you, pray for those who mistreat you. If someone strikes you on one cheek, turn to him the other also. If someone takes your cloak, do not stop him from taking your tunic. Give to everyone who asks you, and if anyone takes what belongs to you, do not demand it back. Do to others as you would have them do to you.

"If you love those who love you, what credit is that to you? Even 'sinners' love those who love them. And if you do good to those who are good to you, what credit is that to you? Even 'sinners' do that. And if you lend to those from whom you expect repayment, what credit is that to you? Even 'sinners' lend to 'sinners', expecting to be repaid in full. But love your enemies, do good to them, and lend to them without expecting to get anything back. Then your reward will be great, and you will be sons of the Most High, because he is kind to the ungrateful and wicked. Be merciful, just as your Father is merciful."[57]

Phrases like "turn the other cheek" and "love your enemies" are commonly used today. This can make it difficult for us to understand the impact of hearing these words for the first time, that day on the "level place" somewhere in Galilee. But this is exactly what we must try to do if we are going to assess the identity of Jesus.

When you think of Christianity in the West, you might think of formal churches with austere atmospheres or extravagant decors. You might think of priests in white robes with gold rings and strange, colourful scarves. But we must cast all of this out of our minds if we are going to appreciate what happened in the Middle East 2,000 years ago. When Jesus taught the crowds, he was a man from the back of beyond standing outdoors in the middle of nowhere, addressing crowds of people with teaching of a kind they'd never heard before.

Much of Jesus' teaching took the form of memorable stories. Some of these are so familiar to us in the West that we fail to notice how brilliant they are. Look closely, for example, at the following parable that Luke records, spoken by Jesus in front of a large crowd:

> "A farmer went out to sow his seed. As he was scattering the seed, some fell along the path; it was trampled on, and the birds of the air ate it up. Some fell on rock, and when it came up, the plants withered because they had no moisture. Other seed fell among thorns, which grew up with it and choked the plants. Still other seed fell on good soil. It came up and yielded a crop, a hundred times more than was sown."
>
> When he said this, he called out, "He who has ears to hear, let him hear."[58]

Later, when Jesus was alone with his disciples, he explained the meaning of the parable for them:

"This is the meaning of the parable: The seed is the word of God. Those along the path are the ones who hear, and then the devil comes and takes away the word from their hearts, so that they may not believe and be saved. Those on the rock are the ones who receive the word with joy when they hear it, but they have no root. They believe for a while, but in the time of testing they fall away. The seed that fell among thorns stands for those who hear, but as they go on their way they are choked by life's worries, riches and pleasures, and they do not mature. But the seed on good soil stands for those with a noble and good heart, who hear the word, retain it, and by persevering produce a crop."[59]

It's a story about how the crowds react to his stories. Even as you listen to it, and try to take in its meaning, the story itself challenges you to listen more closely—to be the "good soil" that hears Jesus' words and bears fruit, rather than being choked by life's worries, riches and pleasures.

But even as we consider the challenge of the parable, let's not forget to assess the man who taught these words. He described the threats anybody would face if they wanted to follow him—times of testing, and life's worries, riches and pleasures—but he made his point using a word-picture that would have been incredibly vivid for his audience. The more we hear of the teaching of Jesus, the less it becomes possible to dismiss him as a fool or a deceiver.

"Love your enemies"; "Do good to those who hate

you"; "Love your neighbour as yourself"; "Blessed are the peacemakers"; "Do to others what you would have them do to you"; "Greater love has no one than this, that he lay down his life for his friends"[60] … the list could go on. The teaching of Jesus remains the basis for our civilization. When things go wrong, we long for people to practise what Jesus taught.

And yet this is the same man who made those outrageous claims about himself. At times his egocentricity was tied directly to his exquisite moral teaching. We cannot separate the two. One day Jesus was asked, "What must we do to do the works God requires?" Jesus answered, "The work of God is this: to believe in the one he has sent".[61] The night before he died, he promised the disciples, "If anyone loves me, he will obey my teaching. My Father will love him, and we will come to him and make our home with him."[62]

It doesn't make sense to conclude that the man who taught these things was a liar who spent his life deceiving people about who he was. Nor is it credible to believe that our entire Western tradition of morality is based on the teaching of a deluded fool. When we find teaching of this ground-breaking, world-changing quality spoken by a man from an insignificant frontier town of the Roman Empire, the best explanation is the one that Jesus gave us himself: that he was not merely a man, but the Son of God.

3. His fulfilment of prophecy

You might be wondering whether this all seems a little bit too random. If there was a God, and he was going to become a man, granted we might expect him to act something like Jesus did. But why wouldn't God make it more obvious? Why wouldn't he announce his arrival a bit more clearly so we could look back on it now and accept that it really was him?

This is where the Old Testament comes in. It was written long before Jesus was born, and we have copies of it that pre-date him. The Old Testament contains many prophecies about God sending his anointed king, the 'Christ', to save his people and rule over the whole world. And quite a number of these prophecies make specific predictions about who this Christ would be, what he would do, where he would be born, and so on.

When we examine the life of Jesus, we find that he fulfils these prophecies with remarkable accuracy. Let us consider a few examples.

It was predicted that the Christ would be in the royal bloodline of David, who was King of Israel sometime around 1000 BC. Matthew, Mark, Luke and John all confirm that Jesus was in this line.[63]

It was predicted that the One to come would be born in Bethlehem, as of course Jesus was.[64] At the time of Jesus' birth, Herod the Great was King of Judea. He was a ruthless ruler who murdered his wife, his three sons, his mother-in-law, brother-in-law and many others. After Jesus was born, King Herod inadvertently fulfilled a prophecy by ordering the killing of babies in Bethlehem.[65] In fulfilment of a different prophecy, Mary and Joseph fled to Egypt to protect Jesus from the genocide.[66]

Before the Christ came, it was prophesied that a messenger would precede him and prepare the way for his work. John the Baptist self-consciously took on this role.[67] Many of the predictions about the Christ are very specific. Although he was to be born in Bethlehem, the Christ was to begin his work in Galilee, in northern Israel.[68] Later in life, he was to enter Jerusalem on a donkey.[69]

In his book *Evidence That Demands a Verdict*, Josh McDowell records 29 prophecies that were fulfilled on the day Jesus died, prophecies written by various people between 1000 BC and 500 BC.[70] The Christ was to be betrayed by a friend for thirty pieces of silver, which would be thrown down in the temple and used to buy a potter's field. He would be abandoned by his disciples and accused by false witnesses. He would be silent before his accusers, wounded and bruised, spat upon and mocked. His hands and his feet would be pierced. He would be crucified with thieves, and he would pray for the persecutors. He would be stared at, and people would shake their heads at him. His garments would be divided up, and they would cast lots for his clothes. His side would be pierced but his bones would not be broken.[71]

Jesus could not have engineered the fulfilment of these predictions, and there are far too many of them for it to be a coincidence. Either Jesus really is the Christ/ King promised by the Old Testament, or we have to reach the unlikely conclusion that Matthew, Mark, Luke and John cooked the whole thing up.

Yet these men suffered greatly for insisting that Jesus was the Christ. Many of the early Christians were killed for what they testified about Jesus. Would they really have died for a lie? Lying in this way would have gone against everything Jesus himself had taught about honesty and integrity. How could they have written these accounts purporting to describe the most inspiring man who has ever lived, while at the same time adding lies to deceive us? We would have to conclude his followers were so captivated by him that they decided to die for a fabricated story about him, but at the same time they were so unimpressed with him that they were prepared to disobey all of his commands about honesty and truth. It does not make sense.

Added to that, the lie would not have worked. As we have noted before, the Gospels were written at a time when people were still alive who knew Jesus and had witnessed his death. If he had not been born in the right town, and worked in the right region, and had the right ancestors, and died under the right circumstances, fulfilling the precise predictions of the Old Testament, then people were around to refute these claims. If the story had been made up, how can we explain the way in which Christianity exploded across the Middle East in the years after Jesus died? Witnesses would have been available to explain that the accounts were not true.

Rather, the fulfilment of these prophecies was a key factor in so many Jewish people becoming followers of

Jesus. They had been waiting for the Christ, and in Jesus they found the man who ticked every box. The coming of God as a man was not a random thing. When Jesus walked the earth, he did so in fulfilment of hundreds of years of prophecy and expectation. The writings of the Old Testament promised this would happen. They act as signposts for us, pointing us to the fact that if God was ever going to come into the world, this is exactly where we would have found him and exactly what he would have done.

4. His miraculous signs

Our next strand of evidence to consider is the claim that Jesus performed miracles. The writers of his biographies recorded these supernatural events as signs of the identity of Jesus. Coming to the end of his book, John writes, "Jesus did many other miraculous signs in the presence of his disciples, which are not recorded in this book. But these are written that you may believe that Jesus is the Christ, the Son of God, and that by believing you may have life in his name."[72]

For example, one day when Jesus was teaching in a house full of people, some men arrived carrying a paralytic man on a mat. They could not get into the house because of the crowd, so they climbed onto the roof and lowered the man on his mat through the tiles and into the middle of the crowd. First, Jesus said to the man, "Friend, your sins are forgiven".[73] It was not that the man was paralysed because of his sin, but rather it was because (as we have already noted) Jesus was demonstrating to the crowd that he had the authority to forgive sins.

But the problem with declaring somebody is forgiven is that it's hard to prove. How would we know whether the man really had been forgiven by God or not? This is where a miraculous sign comes in. Jesus couldn't verify his declaration to be able to forgive sins, but he could verify his authority by making the man walk. Luke records that the religious leaders were angry with Jesus. He goes on:

> Jesus knew what they were thinking and asked,
> "Why are you thinking these things in your hearts?
> Which is easier: to say, 'Your sins are forgiven,' or
> to say, 'Get up and walk'? But that you may know
> that the Son of Man has authority on earth to
> forgive sins …" He said to the paralysed man,
> "I tell you, get up, take your mat and go home."
> Immediately he stood up in front of them, took
> what he had been lying on and went home praising
> God. Everyone was amazed and gave praise to God.
> They were filled with awe and said, "We have seen
> remarkable things today."[74]

The witnesses insist that Jesus performed miracles, and that he did so to establish his identity as the Son of God. But for many of us, miracles are hard to accept. The universe seems to follow established natural laws of cause and effect. For a miracle to happen, those laws would have to be broken. If you've never seen them broken, and if nobody has ever seen them broken under rigorous scientific observation, then perhaps miracles cannot happen.

What, then, are we to make of the supernatural events recorded in the New Testament? First, we need to avoid having a presupposition against the possibility of miracles. I remember once talking to a friend about the evidence that Jesus was raised from the dead. We will examine that evidence in chapter 10, but my friend's response was that Jesus didn't rise from the dead because people don't rise from the dead. This objection is the most common one given against miracles. They cannot have happened because miracles don't happen. It's an argument that will stop us from ever accepting that something supernatural could have occurred, no matter how much evidence we're given. But it's not actually a rational objection to make.

Clearly, the argument begins with the observation that miracles do not happen in the ordinary course of events. It is then argued that because there is such a vast amount of evidence suggesting that miracles do not normally happen, we would need an overwhelming amount of evidence to believe that one ever did.

But this is problematic because of the very nature of miracles. By definition, a 'miracle' is something that strikes us as amazing and extraordinary precisely because it happens so rarely. If 'miracles' happened all the time, they would not be miraculous. They would just be normal, run-of-the-mill happenings. To say that miracles can't occur because they don't occur in most people's experience most of the time is to avoid the question at issue.

102 · NAKED GOD

In fact, if this cosmos isn't all there is, and if there *is* a creator who stands apart from it, then it is quite possible for that creator to act within our universe. Now what if that creator chose to act within our system in such a way as to signal something to us? If miracles happened all the time, then they would signal nothing to us.

CS Lewis put this well. He wrote:

> Nothing can seem extraordinary until you have discovered what is ordinary. Belief in miracles, far from depending on an ignorance of the laws of nature, is only possible in so far as those laws are known. We have already seen that if you begin by ruling out the supernatural you will perceive no miracles. We must now add that you will equally perceive no miracles until you believe that nature works according to regular laws. If you have not yet noticed that the sun always rises in the East you will see nothing miraculous about his rising one morning in the West.[75]

This helps us see through a problem we often feel when we read the first-century accounts of Jesus' life. Many of us have a nagging feeling that people were more gullible back then. They believed in miracles, but we know now that such things do not happen.

However, just because people weren't as scientifically advanced then as we are now, does not mean that they were ignorant of the regular laws of nature. We get a good example of this with the virgin birth. Before Joseph had married Mary, he discovered she was already pregnant. We are told by Matthew what Joseph's immediate reaction was. He decided to call off the engagement. Joseph didn't know as many details about pregnancy as modern doctors do, but he certainly knew enough to know that, normally speaking, women do not get pregnant unless they have had sex with somebody. It was as obvious to Joseph as it is to you and me today, and he reacted exactly as any of us would on hearing the news.

Ultimately, it took the visit of an angel to persuade Joseph that there had been a miracle. When Joseph accepted it, he didn't change his view about what normally happens. Instead, he decided that something very unusual had happened. What had occurred was a complete one-off—the normal pattern of natural laws had been disturbed by God.

What we have now, which Joseph didn't have, is a greater grasp of science. But when you think about it, science has not proved that miracles do not happen— because miracles are by definition an exception to the normal course of things. The New Testament writers knew very well that the miraculous signs they saw were contrary to the normal laws of the world. That is why they recorded them.

In that sense, we are in exactly the same position as they were. Are we prepared to accept the possibility that this ordered universe around us was created? Are we then prepared to accept that such a creator is capable of working within his universe in what to us is a surprising and inexplicable way? And is it not then reasonable to suggest that he would do this for a good reason—such as to establish that, at one point in history, he himself had come into the world?

As we have already established, Jesus was not some random person making a random claim to have super-natural power. After hundreds of years of promises, there came a man who fulfilled all of them with unnerving accuracy. He claimed to be the Son of God. He had the most incredible character in the history of humanity. And he taught as nobody had ever taught before. What I hope has become clear as we have considered these facts, is that this combination of events in itself is nothing other than miraculous. Given what we have already seen about Jesus of Nazareth, would this not be the time when we might expect miracles to happen?

The evidence of those around Jesus is that they did happen. The paralysed man stood up in a crowded room, and everyone was amazed. Everyone was filled with awe. When Jesus calmed a storm with his words, Luke tells us that "in fear and amazement [his disciples] asked one another, 'Who is this? He commands even the winds and the water, and they obey him.'"[76] These are exactly the reactions we would expect.

These are typical examples, in that Jesus performed many of his miracles in front of crowds of witnesses. He turned water into wine at a wedding. He made the blind see and the lame walk. The power he displayed was one of the reasons people travelled from far and wide in their thousands to see him and be healed by him. It is also very striking that his enemies did not deny these miracles were taking place. The best they could do was to try to catch him out by seeing whether he would heal somebody on the Sabbath, the sacred day of rest. They knew he had this power, and they wanted to see if he would break one of their religious rules to use it.

The claim that miracles took place fits credibly with the fact that this was a unique point in history. It does not require us to believe that miracles happen all the time, or even at any other time. The number of witnesses and the unique circumstances surrounding Jesus make the evidence extremely compelling. We, like those first-century witnesses, are faced with a choice. The universe normally obeys natural laws, but will we accept that Jesus had the power to act outside those laws in order to show us that he had the authority and power of God himself?

5. Naked God?

The time has come to draw together these threads of evidence. At the turning point of Mark's Gospel, in chapter 8, Mark records that Jesus took his disciples away and asked them, "Who do people say I am?" Jesus received a variety of answers, because people were still not sure about his identity. Then Jesus asked them, "But what about you? Who do you say I am?"[77] We have seen so far in this book that our answer to Jesus' question is of vital importance to our lives today.

We cannot say that he offers us just one more religious

option among many. Jesus made claims that are impossible to reconcile with other religions. And it is the claims Jesus made about himself that leave us facing a limited number of possibilities as to who he really was.

One common explanation is that Jesus didn't make these claims. On this view, Jesus is a legend. What we have seen is that this does not account for the evidence. All four Gospel writers insist that Jesus made claims to be the Son of God repeatedly throughout his life. Their accounts are written too early to have been falsified, and we have enough copies to indicate that they were not edited or corrupted later.

The fact that Jesus made these claims fits with the historical records of Josephus and Tacitus, who between them confirm he was crucified by Pilate under allegations from the Jewish leaders. The Gospel writers tell us why: the Jewish leaders complained that Jesus was guilty of blasphemy in claiming to be God.

And so as we consider the different strands of evidence, we have to take them together with these astounding claims. Was Jesus lying about himself, or was he a deluded fool? His character emphatically rules out both of these possibilities. He was a truly awesome man: a man of love, balance, humility and compassion.

Neither can his teaching be reconciled with these two options. His moral guidance and insightful parables have touched the hearts of billions of people across the world, from different societies and cultures. It is inconceivable that these teachings were the work of somebody who was either mad or bad.

We have also considered his fulfilment of Old Testament prophecies. These predictions are so specific that they almost look as though the writers were setting themselves up for a fall. How could a man really come and fulfil all of these prophecies? And yet in Jesus we find the man who did.

Finally, we have considered his miraculous signs—events that were witnessed by crowds of ordinary people, and that point to Jesus as a unique figure in the history of the world.

Who was this man? Where will you put your money? Has the cumulative effect of these strands of evidence led you to accept that his claims were true?

His character reassures us that Jesus is a man we can trust. His wisdom confirms that he is a man we can follow. His fulfilment of prophecy affirms that he is exactly what we should have expected. And his miraculous signs indicate that he was no ordinary human being.

It is worth taking stock of the consequences of this. If Jesus was indeed right in claiming that he was the Son of God, then it draws us away from the depressing naked truth of life without God. Jesus teaches us that we were created by God in a special way—that even if God used evolution to form us, he also made us in his image so we could know him and enjoy working for him.

Jesus can fulfil the search for meaning and purpose in our lives, because he teaches us that we were made for a relationship with God. He tells us that there is more to us than our nature and our nurture—that we and the people we know and love are real people, not just complex biological machines. He reveals truth to us, truth about God and truth about ourselves, and gives us confidence that we can know this truth because our minds have more to them than bare evolutionary explanations suggest. And he reassures us of what we already know—that there is a right and wrong in this world, because there is a God who cares about how we treat one another.

The best explanation of the evidence about Jesus is that he was the Son of God. And when we consider the implications of this, it is also the best solution to the problems with naturalism. The naked truth about life without God points us with expectation towards the notion that Jesus' claims were true. In summarizing this position, CS Lewis wrote the following:

> In science we have been reading only the notes to a poem; in Christianity we find the poem itself ... Whether the thing really happened is a historical question. But when you turn to history, you will not demand for it that kind and degree of evidence which you would rightly demand for something intrinsically improbable; only that kind and degree which you demand for something which, if accepted, illuminates and orders all other phenomena, explains both our laughter and our logic, our fear of the dead and our knowledge that it is somehow good to die, and which at one stroke covers what multitudes of separate theories will hardly cover for us if this is rejected.[78]

All that we have considered points us towards a remarkable, life-changing truth. Given the life we would face if there is no God, this is a brilliant discovery. The historical evidence indicates for us that Jesus' claims were true. There is a God, and 2,000 years ago he came into the world as a man. Jesus was God in the flesh.

Jesus was naked God.

CHAPTER 10

DIDN'T JESUS JUST DIE TRAGICALLY YOUNG?

From rock stars to revolutionaries, from President Kennedy to the Princess of Wales, there are numerous examples of high-profile men and women who have died tragically young. Afterwards, their fame has lived and grown. We wonder what they might have gone on to achieve had their lives not been so suddenly stopped short.

Jesus was crucified in his thirties, leaving followers who were devastated. They had come to believe that he really was the long-awaited Christ, and his death must have been all the more difficult to come to terms with in light of his extraordinary character, teachings and actions. Surely if ever there was a man who did not deserve to die young, this was he. And yet there he was, hanging lifeless on a wooden cross.

Yet perhaps the most audacious claim of the early Christians was that Jesus did not stay dead. In this chapter, we will consider this claim and the evidence for it, and the massive implications for us if it is true.

The facts

In considering the resurrection, the first fact to establish is that Jesus was actually dead. We have already seen that Jesus was executed by crucifixion, as the Gospel writers and other sources confirm. After a sham trial and a brutal public flogging, Jesus was hung on a cross, with nails going through his wrists into the horizontal beam. Crucifixion was cruel, painful and effective.

It is important to appreciate that Jesus did in fact die, because one possible alternative explanation for his apparent resurrection is that he didn't die, but fainted from exhaustion and later revived. Jesus was executed under the supervision of Roman soldiers, and one thing Roman soldiers knew how to do was kill people. In this particular case, they were faced with a man who claimed to be the Son of God and the king of the Jews, and who was famous for his miraculous deeds. It was never more important to ensure that a man was definitely dead.

When it looked like Jesus had died, one of the soldiers plunged a spear into his side just to be sure, bringing what John describes as a sudden flow of blood and water. This confirms that Jesus was dead. The physician Alexander Metherell comments, "The spear apparently went through the right lung and into the heart, so when the spear was pulled out, some fluid—the pericardial effusion and the pleural effusion—came out. This would have the appearance of a clear fluid, like water, followed by a large volume of blood, as the eyewitness John described in his gospel."[79]

Once it had been confirmed that Jesus was dead, he was taken down and buried in the tomb of a rich man known as Joseph of Arimathea. The tomb was guarded by Roman soldiers, and the stone covering the tomb was sealed.

Our second fact is that the tomb was found empty. Jesus was crucified on the Friday, and his Jewish followers rested on the following day, that is, the Sabbath. Mark tells us what happened next:

> When the Sabbath was over, Mary Magdalene, Mary the mother of James, and Salome bought spices so that they might go to anoint Jesus' body. Very early on the first day of the week, just after sunrise, they were on their way to the tomb and they asked each other, "Who will roll the stone away from the entrance of the tomb?"[80]

As the women set out to anoint Jesus' dead body with spices, they were expecting to find nothing other than a corpse. Their only concern was that they would not be able to get into the tomb because of the sealed stone entrance. But when they arrived at the burial place, his corpse was missing:

> But when they looked up, they saw that the stone, which was very large, had been rolled away. As they

entered the tomb, they saw a young man dressed in a white robe sitting on the right side, and they were alarmed.

"Don't be alarmed," he said. "You are looking for Jesus the Nazarene, who was crucified. He has risen! He is not here. See the place where they laid him. But go, tell his disciples and Peter, 'He is going ahead of you into Galilee. There you will see him, just as he told you.'"

Trembling and bewildered, the women went out and fled from the tomb. They said nothing to anyone, because they were afraid.[81]

The women saw an angel, who told them Jesus had risen. They reacted in a perfectly understandable way—they were terrified. It's worth noting here that it was women who first witnessed the empty tomb, because this has the ring of truth about it. If it had not happened this way, the Gospel writers would certainly never have made this up. It would have been an awkward fact for those early Christians that it was women rather than men who first found the tomb empty. According to the historian Josephus, the testimony of women was regarded as so unreliable, it was not even allowed in the Jewish courts.[82] As sexist as it might seem to us today, anybody fabricating such a story in the first century would never have chosen women as their first key witnesses.

The women found the tomb empty, and nobody ever produced a body. When Matthew wrote his account of the resurrection, he defended it against a key allegation of the time, which was that the disciples had come and stolen the body of Jesus while the guards were asleep. This is interesting, because it confirms the commonly accepted fact that the tomb was empty. When the Christian faith was exploding across the land, its opponents would only have had to produce the body of Jesus to stop the fledgling movement in its tracks. But nobody ever did, because the body was never found.

Moving on, the third fact we must take into account is that Jesus was seen alive again. He appeared on numerous occasions to various people over a period of weeks following his death.

In one of the earliest New Testament documents, probably written even before the Gospels, the Christian leader Paul wrote the following account to a church in the city of Corinth:

> For what I received I passed on to you as of first
> importance: that Christ died for our sins according
> to the Scriptures, that he was buried, that he was
> raised on the third day according to the Scriptures,
> and that he appeared to Peter, and then to the Twelve.
> After that, he appeared to more than five hundred
> of the brothers at the same time, most of whom are
> still living, though some have fallen asleep.[83]

Not only does Paul record numerous examples of Jesus' resurrection appearances, even one to a crowd of more than 500 people, he also writes this at a time when many of those witnesses were still alive. The Corinthians could have verified Paul's claims by asking the living witnesses to confirm them.

This was no one-off hallucination. Jesus appeared on different occasions to different people. He walked along a road with them, and talked with them. On one occasion he ate a piece of broiled fish in front of them.[84]

When he first appeared to the disciples, one of them, Thomas, was not there. Thomas did not believe the other disciples when they told him about having seen Jesus alive. "Unless I see the nail marks in his hands and put my finger where the nails were, and put my hand into his side, I will not believe it."[85] John records for us what happened next.

> A week later his disciples were in the house again, and Thomas was with them. Though the doors were locked, Jesus came and stood among them and said, "Peace be with you!" Then he said to Thomas, "Put your finger here; see my hands. Reach out your hand and put it into my side. Stop doubting and believe."
>
> Thomas said to him, "My Lord and my God!"
>
> Then Jesus told him, "Because you have seen me, you have believed; blessed are those who have not seen and yet have believed."[86]

As Jesus went on to explain to his disciples, his resurrection appearances fulfilled yet more predictions from the Old Testament about the Christ—that God would not let him decay in the grave, but would raise him to life as the ruler of all.

The evidence for the resurrection is remarkably convincing, especially when you consider the alternatives. If Jesus was not raised from the dead, what happened? He cannot simply have swooned. It is clear enough that he died. It is also quite inconceivable that a man who had been brutally flogged, crucified, and speared through the side should then be able to roll away a massive stone and convince his followers that he was God.

The other major alternative explanation—the body was stolen—is also highly unlikely, given the presence of the guards, the numerous recorded resurrection appearances and the subsequent willingness of the disciples to die for their belief in Jesus' resurrection.

And this brings us on to our fourth and final fact to consider concerning the resurrection. The disciples would have been disillusioned and desperate after seeing their leader killed. Yet within weeks, they went out into the world declaring with remarkable courage and boldness that Jesus was alive again. The zeal of these followers, and their willingness to die for their claims, militates against other possible explanations of the resurrection events. It seems to have been a key factor in persuading the leading Jewish scholar Pinchas Lapide that the resurrection of Jesus really happened:

> When this scared, frightened band of the apostles
> which was just about to throw away everything
> in order to flee in despair to Galilee; when these

peasants, shepherds, and fishermen, who betrayed
and denied their master and then failed him
miserably, suddenly could be changed overnight
into a confident mission society, convinced of
salvation and able to work with much more success
after Easter than before Easter, then no vision or
hallucination is sufficient to explain such a
revolutionary transformation.[87]

About the only argument we are left with against the
resurrection is the one which rules out resurrections as
a matter of presupposition: "The resurrection didn't
happen because resurrections don't happen". But as we
found when we considered the miracles of Jesus, the fact
that resurrections do not normally happen does not prove
one way or the other whether this particular resurrection
happened. The New Testament doesn't ask us to believe
that people get resurrected all the time, but that when
God came into our world as a man, and was crucified, he
rose from the dead.

Once we remove the presupposition and look objectively
at the facts, I think it actually takes more faith *not* to
believe the resurrection story than to believe it.

Lord Darling was at one time the Lord Chief Justice,
the most senior criminal law judge in Britain. Having seen
his fair share of trials, he wrote that "there exists such
overwhelming evidence, positive and negative, factual
and circumstantial, that no intelligent jury in the world
could fail to bring in a verdict that the resurrection story
is true".[88]

The implications

We must now consider the far-reaching implications of Jesus' resurrection from the dead. Of course, we can start with what this adds to our picture of Jesus' identity. The overwhelming evidence for the resurrection is another arrow pointing us to the truth of Jesus' claim to be the Son of God.

But there is more to the resurrection than that. First, it shows us that Jesus is the champion over death. It proves for us that death is not the end. Jesus' resurrection offers us the hope that one day there can be life after death for everyone.

Jesus promised this. He said to Martha, one of his followers and friends, "I am the resurrection and the life. He who believes in me will live, even though he dies; and whoever lives and believes in me will never die. Do you believe this?"[89] By his own resurrection, Jesus has proved that this incredible claim is not a cruel lie to give people false hope. The resurrection confirms he was speaking the truth.

It is hard to grasp how brilliant this is. Whatever you choose to live for, death will bring an end to it. The reality of our own death means that we will soon be forgotten. We will die, and our great-great-grandchildren, if we have them, will probably not even know our names.

Of course, far worse than that and as you probably already know, death will take away the people you love the most. Even to give examples from real life almost seems too much to bear. This is another area where experience tells us something that theoretical knowledge never can. In chapter 9 we looked at the scene in *Good Will Hunting* where Sean Maguire pointed out Will's lack of life experience. Sean goes on:

> "You're a tough kid. I ask you about war, you'd probably throw Shakespeare at me, right? 'Once more unto the breach dear friends.' But you've never been near one. You've never held your best friend's head in your lap, and watch him gasp his last breath looking to you for help. I ask you about love, you'd probably quote me a sonnet. But you've never looked at a woman and been totally vulnerable, known someone that could level you with her eyes, feeling like God put an angel on earth just for you, who could rescue you from the depths of hell. And you wouldn't know what it's like to be her angel, to have that love for her, be there forever, through anything, through cancer. And you wouldn't know about sleeping sitting up in a hospital room for two months, holding her hand, because the doctors could see in your eyes that the terms 'visiting hours' don't apply to you. You don't know about real loss because it only occurs when you love something more than you love yourself. And I doubt you've ever dared to love anybody that much."

Death is a horrible thing. But the resurrection shows us the amazing truth that in Jesus Christ, death is not the end. Jesus was raised from the dead, because he is the champion over it.

The second implication of the resurrection is that it shows us that Jesus is the ruler over the world. The same man who lived that life of love in the Middle East has risen to reign over all. This is part of what it means for Jesus to be God's promised 'Christ' or king. According to the Old Testament, when the Christ came in the royal line of King David, he would sit on David's throne—not just to rule over Israel, but to bring justice and good government to the whole world. There are lots of men and women in the world today who have power and control over property and people, but ultimately there is no authority anywhere in the world that is not subject to the risen, ruling Jesus Christ. This transforms the way we are to understand Jesus and his teaching. When Jesus taught us how to live, he was not just passing on some helpful advice that we could take or leave. He is our rightful ruler, and he was telling us what should go on and what should not go on in his world. We do not have the right to ignore him. We do not have autonomy or independence from him. And in the end, we will be answerable to him.

Jesus taught that the way we live matters because there will be a judgement day. Everyone who has ever lived will be held to account, because we have a risen ruler who loves the world and cares about justice.

This is exactly how those early followers of Jesus understood his resurrection. When they travelled far and wide, suffering to death so they could tell others about Jesus, the rule or lordship of Jesus was intrinsic to their message. One of those men, Paul, preached the message in Athens, and made this startling challenge to his audience:

> "In the past God overlooked such ignorance, but
> now he commands all people everywhere to
> repent. For he has set a day when he will judge the
> world with justice by the man he has appointed.
> He has given proof of this to all men by raising him
> from the dead."[90]

Jesus is the risen ruler, with authority over us. He will return to judge us all. He cannot be ignored. As modern people, we may be used to thinking that Jesus is just another religious option or historical figure to investigate and consider, and that it is up to us what we do with him. But the resurrection puts us in the uncomfortable position of not having this option. Jesus is not just another historical figure we can take or leave. If he is the risen Christ, then we are living in his world and, whether we like it or not, he is going to judge us for how we live.

Of course, the fact that Jesus will return to judge the world is actually wonderful news. It takes only a moment's thought about our own personal experience or the wider world to appreciate how much we long for there to be justice. We get rightly angry when we hear of people unjustly hurting or abusing others. It happens on every level. The teenagers at a school who pretended to befriend a disabled classmate, then took her to a playground in the pouring rain, removed the wheels from her wheelchair and left her. The soldiers who tortured and humiliated their captives in the Abu Ghraib prison. Josef Fritzl, who kept his daughter Elisabeth captive for 24 years in a purpose-built cell and fathered seven children with her, three of whom grew up in the cellar without sunlight.

We long for justice. And it's clear from the teaching of Jesus that he is even more passionate about justice than we are. The wonderful news about the resurrection is that Jesus is the man who will do something about it. Jesus Christ can do what we are powerless to do ourselves. He promised that one day he will hold people to account. It will be true justice, because Jesus knows the actions and motivations of everyone. God the Father knows who is responsible, and he cares enough to have appointed Jesus Christ to ensure that justice will be done. Gary Haugen, the Director of the International Justice Mission, writes this:

> … the knowledge of God's great anger toward and condemnation of injustice is what gives me hope to seek justice in this world. Standing with my boots deep in the reeking muck of a Rwandan mass grave where thousands of innocent people have been horribly slaughtered, I have no words, no meaning, no life, no hope if there is not a God of history and time who is absolutely outraged, absolutely furious, absolutely burning with anger toward those who took it into their own hands to commit such acts.[91]

We have seen in this chapter the extraordinary facts that demonstrate the historical reality of Jesus' resurrection. They show us that Jesus is the champion over death, so we can have confidence that death is not the end. And they also show us that Jesus is the ruler of the world, so we can look forward to a day when he judges everybody with true, informed, impartial justice.

Jesus is the risen ruler. We will all be held to account for how we have responded to him and his teaching. It is terrific news for any of us who want justice. But you might already have been thinking of some problems with this. In the next two chapters we will consider some potential problems with living in a world where Jesus is the ruler.

CHAPTER 11

THREE COMMON
PROBLEMS

By looking at the evidence about Jesus, we are being led to some amazing conclusions. In the last chapter, we considered the facts surrounding his resurrection. One of the implications of the resurrection story is that Jesus is not just an historical figure. He is the living ruler of the world, who has promised to one day bring the justice that we all long to see.

In this chapter, we will consider three potential problems with this. You might feel these objections very strongly. For many who decide to reject the Bible's claims about Jesus, it is less that they don't believe it and more that they can't bring themselves to believe it. If it were all true, the implications are just too undesirable.

Let's look at three common examples.

Isn't his teaching socially regressive?

Kate was a friend of mine who came with me to a course being run at my church called *Christianity Explored*. After we'd done most of the course, I asked Kate what she was making of it all. She said, "The thing is, I've never really had any doubt that Jesus was who he said he was. But I can't take it any further than that, because I can't accept what he teaches about sex."

Kate's problem, and it is a common one, was that some of Jesus' teaching offended her own ideas of right and wrong. A colleague of mine once said to me that the Bible could not be true because it states that women and men are not equal. The issue here is really the same. How can we be prepared to accept Jesus as the ruling Son of God if we find that his teaching is primitive, backward or socially regressive?

Tim Keller, author of *The Reason for God*,[92] has worked for over 20 years as the pastor of a church in Manhattan, and has helped thousands of people who have voiced objections of this kind.

Keller's first piece of advice is that we should work hard to understand what Jesus actually said, in his original context. For example, when we chase up what the Bible really says about men and women (rather than the common caricature of it), we find that the Bible strongly affirms the equality of the sexes, while also teaching that men and women are different. On the face of it, that's hard to disagree with. Most of us would accept that there are significant differences between men and women. But if we hear some sentences from the Bible about women quoted in isolation, it may seem as though the Bible is saying that women are inferior to men. We need to put in the work to understand what the whole Bible teaches, not just a snippet taken out of context. The equality of men and women is emphasized from the very first chapter of the Bible. If we work hard to understand the context in this way, we often find that we actually agree with Jesus' teaching far more than we had originally thought.

But what if we find Jesus' teaching unacceptable even after we've read carefully to understand what he meant? Tim Keller then suggests we need to guard against our own cultural imperialism—that is, the assumption that our culture and our view must be superior and right. We easily forget that we ourselves have a context.

We have an historical context. Just as our grandparents believed things that we would be embarrassed about, so our grandchildren will look back on some of our cherished beliefs and shake their heads. These things move quickly. There are probably things you believed ten years ago that you look back on now and think are clearly wrong. Who is to say the same won't happen in ten years' time about your opinions now? And this is all just over a lifetime. What if our society spends the whole 21st century clinging to certain values of right and wrong that by the 31st century people regard as completely backward and regressive?

We also have a geographical and cultural context. Imagine that you asked people in Melbourne or Chicago or

London to list the parts of Jesus' teaching they find offensive. Then imagine that you went to some other parts of the world and did the same—people in the Middle East, and West Africa, and Southwest China. Of course the objections would be entirely different. Some people might be offended by Jesus' attitude towards sex, but be attracted by his commandments about love. Others would wholeheartedly agree with Jesus' teaching on sex, but would argue that it's totally unworkable and ridiculous to love our enemies.

Even where we feel very strongly that Jesus teaches something we disagree with, it is dangerous simply to assume that we are right and Jesus must be wrong. Who is to say that our objections to Jesus' teaching are the important ones, given that other people in other places or at other times have raised objections to aspects of Jesus' teaching that don't bother us at all?

Jesus claimed to be teaching God's truth for all societies at all times. Jesus will have said things that go against what the majority think in any one society at any one time. It would be wrong to reject him simply because, on certain issues, we don't like what he said. It assumes that we definitely have things right, and forgets that we have a particular context.

Of course we all probably accept that if we were able to have a conversation with the all-knowing creator of the universe, there would be plenty of ways in which our moral values might not line up with his. In that sense, when we encounter Jesus in the New Testament, we get exactly what we should expect. We might find some of his teaching hard to take, but that's because of who he was. Is it so surprising that when God comes into our world, we should find ourselves having to adjust some of our cherished opinions in light of his teaching?

Don't his followers have a disgraceful track record?

The next problem to deal with is the appalling behaviour of some people who claim to follow Jesus. History is littered with indefensible atrocities committed in the name of Jesus Christ. Perhaps closer to home, you might know people who profess to be Christians but whose behaviour is utterly unattractive.

There are two points to make. The first, and more minor point, is that it is extremely difficult in these cases to compare like with like. When we meet somebody who claims to be a Christian, we might well find that they are not nearly as pleasant to be around as people we know who aren't Christian. But often, the comparison we're making is unfair. We all know that some people come from stable loving family backgrounds and it often results in them being stable loving people. Other people have had very troubled backgrounds and sometimes it can be reflected in their character.

Before we jump too quickly to conclusions about the behaviour of Christian people, we should find out what they were like *before* they came to Christ. Over time—and developments in somebody's character are always slow— have they changed?

The Bible says we should look for things like whether people have become more loving towards others. Are they more patient and kind? Are they more self-controlled and gentle? The fair test of the effect on an individual of their relationship with Jesus Christ is to compare them with how they were before that change.

Of course, this still leaves many people who claim to follow Jesus Christ but who live in a pretty awful way. The second and more fundamental answer to this problem is to assess Jesus by himself and not by his alleged followers. By looking at the teaching of Jesus Christ, we can ask: What would Jesus have thought of that person's behaviour? Is it an authentic Christlike lifestyle, or not?

The story is told of a Christian man named Yakov who was trying to share his faith with an older man named Cimmerman. When he tried to bring Jesus into the conversation, Cimmerman said, "Don't talk to me about Christ! You see those priests there, with all their vestments, all of their cloaks, all of the big crosses on their chests? I know what they're like. They're violent people. They have abused their power. Don't tell me about Christ! I know what it is like to watch them kill our people, even some of my own relatives."

Yakov told Cimmerman a story. He said, "What if I stole your coat and your boots, put them on, broke into a bank and stole the money? I was chased by the police but I outran them. What would you say if the police came knocking on your door and charged you with breaking into a bank?"

Cimmerman said he would deny it, but Yakov asked

how he would react when the police said they knew it must be him because they had recognized his coat and his boots.

The conversation didn't get much further, but Cimmerman had understood Yakov's point. Over time, Yakov built up a friendship with Cimmerman in which he lived, as far as he could, an authentic Christian life. Eventually Cimmerman asked him one day, "Yakov, tell me about this Christ that you so love and live for. How can I know him?" After Yakov had explained, and Cimmerman committed his life to Jesus Christ, Cimmerman embraced Yakov and said, "Thank you for being in my life. You wear his coat very well."[93]

We might find that in our lives, we come across people who claim to be Christians, but who are more like Cimmerman's priests with their hatred and hypocrisy. But we must not allow such people to distort our view of Jesus Christ. They might wear his coat and boots, but they are impostors. We must go back to Jesus himself in the New Testament, and assess him there.

Won't he take away my freedom?

The third objection to consider is whether accepting Jesus will restrict our freedom and our lifestyle. Do you ever look at Christians and think they are trapped? At the moment you're living how you want to live, but if you decide to follow Jesus you won't be free to do that anymore. Inevitably there will be times when Jesus will want you to live a certain way, or make a certain decision, and you won't want to. Wouldn't it be better just to be free to live how we like? Well, let's consider what Jesus said about this.

> To the Jews who had believed him, Jesus said, "If you hold to my teaching, you are really my disciples. Then you will know the truth, and the truth will set you free."
>
> They answered him, "We are Abraham's descendants and have never been slaves of anyone. How can you say that we shall be set free?"
>
> Jesus replied, "I tell you the truth, everyone who sins is a slave to sin. Now a slave has no permanent place in the family, but a son belongs to it forever. So if the Son sets you free, you will be free indeed."[94]

Jesus offended these Jewish followers because he said that if they followed him, they would know the truth and the truth would set them free. They were surprised, because they weren't slaves. Perhaps the same goes for us. We're not slaves, so how can Jesus claim that following him will set us free?

But Jesus responded by saying that it's our 'freedom' that enslaves us. "I tell you the truth, everyone who sins is a slave to sin." We will consider more carefully what Jesus meant by the word 'sin' in our next chapter, but a helpful definition for now is that sin is living our own way instead of God's way. Sin is deciding not to submit to Jesus as our king, but to live the way we want to. The surprise here is that Jesus turns our objection on its head, and teaches that if we sin we cease to be free.

This is because sin is a rebellion not only against God but against reality. God made the world a certain way. He made fish, for example, to swim in water. Is a fish 'free' if it decides to exit the water and flop about on the land? In the way we often use the word 'freedom', it would be. It has exercised a free choice, and is refusing to be confined to what other people have decided is the 'right' place for fish. We see freedom, in other words, as the completely unrestricted choice of the individual to do absolutely anything.

But we are only free when we live in accordance with who we were made to be. Birds are free when they fly, and fish when they swim, and humans when they love God and live as God created us to live. When we choose to live in defiance of this reality—in defiance of how the world works and is to be enjoyed—we find ourselves trapped. Things go wrong. We make still further choices that we hope will fix things, but they only dig the hole deeper. And we discover in the end that our assertion of 'freedom' has left us with all the options and success of a fish out of water.

Jesus warns that in this sense, to choose sin is to choose slavery. We think we're free if we don't choose to follow him, but we're not. And it this slavery that stops us from turning to Jesus and following his teaching. We might not want to obey what Jesus teaches about money because we are slaves to the destructive materialism of our society, which sees happiness as a product our money can buy. We might not want to obey what Jesus teaches about sex because we are slaves to the happiness we think we can get (but somehow never quite achieve) by pursuing sensual

134 · NAKED GOD

pleasure. There comes a point when we don't want to obey Jesus because we are slaves to something else.

Jesus offers the true freedom that the fish experiences when it jumps back in the water. He promises that his truth will set us free: the truth that there is a God, and that we were made to relate to him and work for him. We long for purpose and meaning in our lives, and these longings find their fulfilment in knowing God. That's what we were made for.

Against that, in Part I we considered the depressing realities of what this universe would be like if there was no God. In January 2009, an atheist advertising campaign was launched on buses across London and other cities. The slogan was, 'There's probably no God. Now stop worrying and enjoy your life.' As we have uncovered the truth about Jesus Christ, we have seen that there is a God, because the evidence demonstrates that God came to earth as a man. But we also need to think critically about the second half of the atheist slogan. If there really is no God, we would be nothing more than machines in a meaningless universe where there is no right or wrong. The slogan makes it sound as though life without God would be enjoyable, and it appeals because it sounds liberating. But Jesus warned us that if we reject him, we will only bind ourselves in slavery to something else.

Against all of this, Jesus drew the analogy of becoming a child of God: "Now a slave has no permanent place in the family, but a son belongs to it forever". He promised that if we choose to follow him, we won't be slaves. Instead, we become children of God. We were made for that relationship with God, and Jesus came so we could enjoy that relationship again. If we choose to do this, we will find true freedom.

IN THIS CHAPTER WE HAVE CONSIDERED THREE possible problems with accepting Jesus as our ruler and following him. All three of these issues are very common, and they can get in the way of us accepting the truth about Jesus Christ. But I hope you can see that, on closer examination, they are not legitimate objections.

However, we will now turn to consider the real problem with Jesus Christ being the risen ruler of the world. This problem concerns what we are really like, and the way we have treated God. We have considered the naked truth of life without God, and we have considered the truth about the historical Christ. We must now turn to expose the truth about ourselves.

PART III

NAKED YOU

CHAPTER 12

THE ONE REAL PROBLEM

IN OUR LAST CHAPTER, WE LOOKED AT SOME common problems people have with Jesus. In this chapter, I want to spend some time thinking about a more fundamental problem that everyone has with Jesus—although many of us may not realize it.

Put simply the problem is this: if Jesus is indeed the risen ruler of the world who will one day judge us all, how are people like you and me going to fare when we stand before him? When Jesus comes to right all the wrongs in the world, will one of the 'wrongs' be me, and my behaviour towards other people?

There are actually two different ways to be found guilty before God, and every one of us fails in at least one of those ways. When we look at the teaching of Jesus, this comes as a great surprise to many people. I used to think Christians believed there were two kinds of people in the world—good people who followed Jesus, and bad people who didn't. That's not what Christians believe. When we look at what Jesus said, we see that there are indeed two kinds of people in the world, but neither of them is good.

1. People who drink from broken cisterns

600 years before Jesus was born, there was a prophet called Jeremiah. His basic job was to explain to his own generation that they were guilty before God. His words, now contained in the Old Testament, include the following message from God:

> "My people have committed two sins:
> They have forsaken me,
>   the spring of living water,
> and have dug their own cisterns,
>   broken cisterns that cannot hold water."[95]

Water from a good spring is clean, full of minerals and essential for life, which I guess is why so many of us carry around bottles of it these days. God is saying here that he is a life-giving spring of water for his people.

Jesus also applied this image to himself (as we saw in chapter 8). At a Jewish festival he said, "If anyone is thirsty, let him come to me and drink. Whoever believes in me, as the Scripture has said, streams of living water will flow from within him."[96] God can provide us with everything we need. He invites us to live in a relationship with him, knowing him, working for him and enjoying the good things he gives us. He promises that if we live like this, in the relationship we were made for, we will find our true purpose. We will be truly alive.

God's people in the time of Jeremiah had forsaken the spring of living water and had dug their own cisterns instead. Cisterns are big tanks or containers that you use to store rain water. They can be extremely useful in places where water is scarce.

But here's the strange thing about this story. You don't need cisterns in a place where there is a flowing, healthy spring. If there's nothing wrong with your water supply, there's no need to dig a cistern and collect the rain. You only dig a cistern if (for some reason) you don't want to use the spring.

This is what God's people had done, and it is also what we all do. We live in God's world, but we choose not to depend on him or go to him as the source of all that is life-giving and good. Instead, we dig our own cisterns. We serve other masters. We live for other 'gods', and look to them to satisfy our needs and desires.

This is what we saw in our last chapter, when we discussed whether Jesus would take away our freedom. Jesus explained that when we choose to reject him (that is, to 'sin') we find ourselves enslaved to a different master. We serve something that we think will make us happy. Different people serve different things. Some people are focused on their family; others on friendships; others make sacrifices to get success at work; still others strive to make money. We think that once we get that thing, then we will be free.

People often think this in particular about making money. "If I can only get to that level", they think to themselves, "then I can stop work and live it up!" But making money is strangely seductive—the more you make, the more you think you need. It's very hard to reach the point when you think you have enough. And even if you do stop making sacrifices to make money, you will just serve something else. Something else will seduce you into thinking that it is the source of true happiness—holidays or experiences or a relationship. We are always looking to something, and serving something, hoping it will satisfy us. And in choosing something else to serve, we choose not to serve God.

The trouble is, these alternative sources of life just don't work. As Jeremiah puts it, they are "broken cisterns that cannot hold water". We think they will satisfy us, but they never do. That's why people constantly ask, "Is there more to life than this?" It is why, no matter how many of our ambitions we achieve, we always want more. The cisterns promise so much, but they do not hold water. And in the meantime, the living water we long for and need is flowing from the spring we have rejected.

It's not that God wants to spoil our fun. God only wants us to do what's best for us—to turn back to him, to depend on him, to serve him. He wants us to treat him as God, in other words, and to live as his people, because he is the source of life-giving water.

Turning away from God to our own broken cisterns is not only ineffective in the long run; it is also just plain wrong. Jeremiah describes it as a "sin". It is offensive to God. He made us for a relationship with him, and we have turned away because we think we can be happier if we live for other things. This is God's complaint against his people in Jeremiah's time. I've done everything for you, says God. I've created you, and rescued you, and provided for you time and again. And yet you turn away from me, and the life-giving water I give.

God is only asking for what he deserves. He is the creator of the universe and the source of everything that is good. He deserves to be recognized and thanked for that. When an Olympic athlete wins a gold medal, we don't begrudge her the chance to stand on the podium and receive her award. It's exactly what she has earned. Likewise, when God asks us to relate to him and honour him, it is absolutely right for us to do so.

In the movie *One Hour Photo*, Seymour Parrish lives a lonely life developing photographs in a department store. Seymour becomes obsessed with the Yorkin family, who have been getting their photos developed by him for years. His obsession becomes increasingly sinister as the movie unfolds.

One day, when the Yorkins are out of the house, Seymour breaks in. Right from the moment Seymour enters the home, there is high tension. He is walking around in their house without permission, and it's just not right.

And Seymour is in no rush as he explores the house he

has seen in their photos for years. He goes into their son's bedroom. He uses their toilet. He takes a beer from their fridge. He sits on their sofa and watches a baseball game. In short, he treats the house as if it's his own. And all the time, as you watch, there is the nerve-wracking reality that this is not his house, and the owner is coming back.

It's a chilling picture. Seymour's behaviour would have been fine if it was his house, but it's not his house and he is disregarding the true owner. It is even more chilling when we realize that we have treated God just like Seymour treated the Yorkins. We live in his world as though it's our own, ignoring the true owner as though he will never come back.[97]

All of this helps us understand what the Bible means by the much misunderstood word 'sin'. Sin is not about the 'seven deadly sins', or those things that are 'naughty but nice', like getting drunk or eating chocolate. Fundamentally, we sin when we don't let God be God—when we turn away from him and live for something else instead.

This is the first way that people are guilty before God, and it leaves us facing a horrendous problem. Jesus Christ is the risen ruler, and we live in a world that belongs to him. And so if we live in his world, but rebel against his kind, gracious, rightful reign, we are setting ourselves up for a confrontation we cannot hope to win.

When Jesus comes to judge, he will do it with complete, perfect justice. The creator of the universe will put right every wrong. The problem we all face is that the way we have treated God makes us one of those 'wrongs' that needs to be put right. We are guilty of turning our backs on the fountain of living water, and we face his judgement. Even if we resolve to turn back to the spring of living water now, somebody will have to make good the damage we have caused.

Before we think further about how this might be achieved, we need to outline the other way that people tend to reject God.

2. People who take refuge in religion

What we have looked at so far should seem clear enough, even if it is disturbing. If we accept that Jesus is the Son of God, it follows on naturally that we have a real problem if we do not live with him as the ruler of our lives.

But the second way to find ourselves guilty before God might come as more of a surprise. It is what we might call the 'religious' way.

Lots of people who do try to follow God think of him a bit like Father Christmas. With Father Christmas, the tradition is that he knows if you've been bad or good, and you get presents from him if you've been sufficiently good. I've never actually met anyone who was denied their presents as a child because they hadn't been good, but the threat is still there. The presents seem to be a reward from Santa Claus for being a good kid the rest of the year.

This understanding of good and bad is the basis for a lot of religion. The argument goes that there is a line separating good people from bad people, and we need to get above that line. People below the line are not good enough to please God, and they'll be guilty on the judgement day. But if you can get yourself above the line, then Jesus will be satisfied that you've put in a good effort, and will reward you.

The way you get above the line is to do the kind of things that will impress God—helping old ladies across the street, giving to charity, and of course being involved in religious activities like getting your children baptized or going to church. We might not be perfect, and there might be people who are a bit better than us, but it's all about making the cut.

When we come to the teaching of Jesus, we find that this form of religion does not work. The problem is that we will never be good enough to make the cut. This is because the standard required is much more penetrating and demanding than we often admit. Jesus once said:

> "Be on your guard against the yeast of the Pharisees, which is hypocrisy. There is nothing concealed that will not be disclosed, or hidden that will not be made known. What you have said in the dark will be heard in the daylight, and what you have whispered in the ear in the inner rooms will be proclaimed from the roofs."[98]

Jesus' words leave us in no doubt about how uncomfortable we will feel on that day of judgement. Our external appearances might be all right. We might have impressed people by our church attendance or little-old-lady-helping.

But God sees everything. Everything we've ever said in secret will be heard in the open. Everything we've ever done or thought will be disclosed. And the person who will weigh these thoughts, words and actions will be none other than Jesus Christ, the most good, true, honest, pure, holy person imaginable.

If we are tempted to think that we might pass his test, it's usually because we don't appreciate how good he really is. We compare ourselves to other people, and we might think that we do pretty well. But Jesus will judge humanity from his perspective, not ours. And his standards are way beyond ours.

I don't know if you've ever been in a position where you've suddenly found out that the standards are much higher than you'd realized. When I was a teenager, I played the cello to what I thought was a pretty high standard. I was the leader of the cello section in my school orchestra, and we kept winning awards. I was in my county youth orchestra, and we'd been on tours around Europe.

In the summer before I went to university, I heard about a scholarship that was available for a few of the very best musicians. I decided I should apply for the scholarship. I thought I stood a pretty good chance, and my teacher thought so too. So I made the application, prepared a piece and went down to Cambridge for my audition.

On the way, if you'd asked me whether I was good at the cello, I'd have been pretty confident that I was. Compared to every other cellist I'd heard, I was doing fine. But when I arrived for the audition, I got a very uncomfortable shock.

Even in the waiting room, while people were practising, I realized there had been some sort of mistake. The people I heard were of a standard I'd never imagined teenagers could be. They were prodigies. They had prepared their pieces for many months, and some of them had been taught by the world's very best musicians. When I went into the audition, it confirmed what had already dawned on me. The standard they wanted was higher than I had ever imagined. When I finished hacking away at Beethoven for five minutes, struggling to keep pace with the professional pianist who accompanied me, I looked at the faces of the adjudication panel. I could tell what they were thinking. How on earth had I ended up applying for this scholarship? It was a hugely embarrassing experience.

I thought I was worthy of the scholarship, but only because I had massively underestimated the standard. Now, discovering that you're not a very good musician is no big deal. But to make the same mistake about your standing before God would be catastrophic.

This is absolutely critical to understand. We must appreciate that when we stand before Jesus and give an account for the life we have lived, he will be completely justified in finding us guilty. In fact, God would not be perfect himself if he said that we were good enough.

God cares about wrongdoing far more than we can imagine. It's not just murder that matters to him, because getting angry is wrong as well. It's not just rape that matters to him, because lust is wrong as well. Pride and greed and envy are wrong, and we know in our heart that they are. God is so loving and so good that he will ensure that none of these wrongs committed in his universe goes unpunished.

This is the problem with trying to obtain a 'not guilty' verdict from God through our own religious merit. None of us are good enough. When faced with a day of judgement, Alexander Solzhenitsyn summed up our condition brilliantly. He wrote, "If only there were evil people somewhere insidiously committing evil deeds, and it were necessary only to separate them from the rest of us and destroy them. But the line dividing good and evil cuts through the heart of every human being."[99]

WE HAVE SEEN THAT THERE ARE TWO WAYS THAT WE all respond to God, but that both of them end up with a 'guilty' verdict. The first way is to reject God and serve other things instead. The second way is to try to be good and keep religious rules, but this fails because we are never good enough.

In either case, when we stand before Jesus on that day of reckoning, he will be completely justified if he finds us guilty.

Where does that leave us?

CHAPTER 13

BREAKTHROUGH

IN THE MOVIE *Brassed Off*, THE STORY IS TOLD OF A mining community in the north of England who face the threat of unemployment. Gloria is a young woman who arrives in the town and joins the Grimley Brass Band, the heart and soul of the town. She is working for the government and writing a report on the financial viability of the mine.

As the story progresses, and friendships are formed between Gloria and the local miners, the time comes for her to submit her report. She has made a case for the ongoing future of the mine, but when she hands it in, there is a terrible twist. The government has already made the decision to close the mine, and will not pay any attention to Gloria's report.

It's a strange moment in the movie, because you realize that there was no point in Gloria ever coming to the mining town at all. She was asked to write a report, but the decision had already been made. Her time in Grimley achieved nothing for the community.

At this point in the book, you'd be forgiven for wondering whether it was equally pointless that Jesus ever came into the world. His character impresses us and his teaching convicts us and his resurrection proves that he is the Lord. But if we've all turned away from the living God, and we are all guilty before him, what was the point of Jesus coming?

Most people answer this question by assuming that Jesus came to tell us all to try harder, to be better, to somehow make the grade by obeying the rules. But nothing could be further from the truth. According to Jesus, we will never be able to stand on our two feet before God and make the grade.

So why did Jesus come?

The wish that was granted

We begin to understand the answer to our question when we notice who Jesus spent his time with. Jesus did not hang around with the devout religious people—the religious leaders and do-gooders of the day. He socialized with tax collectors, who everybody knew were corrupt swindlers. He befriended prostitutes. He helped a Samaritan woman who was with a new man after having five different husbands. If Jesus' standards were so high, why did he spend most of his time with people who everyone else thought of as so low?

The basic answer is that Jesus didn't come to give religious people a pat on the back, or to tell everyone to try harder. He came to bring mercy and forgiveness for sinful, guilty people. When the religious leaders of his day criticized Jesus for hanging around with blatantly sinful people, Jesus' answer was this: "It is not the healthy who need a doctor, but the sick. I have not come to call the righteous, but sinners."[100]

On another occasion Jesus told a story that beautifully illustrates the point:

> To some who were confident of their own righteousness and looked down on everybody else, Jesus told this parable: "Two men went up to the temple to pray, one a Pharisee and the other a tax collector. The Pharisee stood up and prayed about himself: 'God, I thank you that I am not like other men—robbers, evildoers, adulterers—or even like this tax collector. I fast twice a week and give a tenth of all I get.'
>
> "But the tax collector stood at a distance. He would not even look up to heaven, but beat his breast and said, 'God, have mercy on me, a sinner.'
>
> "I tell you that this man, rather than the other, went home justified before God. For everyone who exalts himself will be humbled, and he who humbles himself will be exalted."[101]

The Pharisees were devoutly religious people, and the man in Jesus' story was no exception. Jesus makes clear that the man kept a lot of religious rules. In his fasting and his giving, he even goes beyond the rules people thought were essential at the time. His prayer is self-centred. He talks to God about everything he has achieved. It's "me, me, me". His prayer is also self-righteous—he thinks that on his own, he has done enough to stand before God without needing forgiveness. He asks nothing of God. All he can do is thank God that he is not like those 'other' people.

We need to think of a modern equivalent of this man to give the story its true impact. This is an archbishop or a priest or an upright church-going pillar of the community. The world sees him as very religious and moral, but it turns out that he is proud and self-righteous. For all the reasons we looked at in the last chapter, his own religious efforts are not enough to get him right with God.

But what about the second man? He has lived his life with his back turned on God. He is a tax collector, and again we need to think of a modern equivalent. This is a serious criminal—the sort of criminal that people would be genuinely appalled to hear could ever be forgiven. He's the kind of con-man who cheats the elderly out of their life savings. He's the collaborator who got rich helping the Nazis during the war. And of course, this man is not right with God either.

Neither man deserves anything but judgement. But then Jesus tells us that the tax collector went home justified before God. He was forgiven by God for the way he had lived, because he was prepared to humble himself. He was genuinely contrite about the way he had lived, and so he begged God for mercy. He wanted to turn his life around. He realized his need and cried out, "God, have mercy on me, a sinner".

We could never be 'justified' before God by ourselves. The incredible news Jesus brings is that, like the tax collector, we can be right with God if we turn back to him in humility and beg his forgiveness.

But how is that possible?

The great exchange

We considered in the last chapter the difficulty with forgiving sinful people—that if on that final judgement day God were to overlook our wrongdoing, he would be saying that human evil doesn't matter to him. God cannot and will not do that, because he is just and holy and good, and wants to see justice done in his universe.

And this is why Jesus came. The amazing news is that Jesus didn't just come to tell us we were condemned. He came to earth to provide the means by which anybody, no matter who they are and what they have done, can be forgiven and can turn back to God.

We can see already why this is the most wonderful news. After the frightening reality check in our last chapter about what all of us really deserve, we now find that God has provided a way for us to be completely forgiven. What is all the more amazing is the step God took to make it all possible. He decided to deal with the problem himself, by sending his Son to die.

When Jesus' followers began to understand that he was the Christ, the great king, he immediately started to tell them that he had come to die. Referring to himself as the 'Son of Man', a phrase used in the Old Testament about the Christ, Mark tells us that Jesus "began to teach them that the Son of Man must suffer many things and be rejected by the elders, chief priests and teachers of the law, and that he must be killed and after three days rise again".[102]

Jesus didn't just die as an example for us—although his death is indeed an extraordinary example of love and sacrifice for the sake of others. His death wasn't a gesture or an act of martyrdom. His death achieved something, and Jesus knew in advance that it would. He once said to his disciples: "For even the Son of Man did not come to be served, but to serve, and to give his life as a ransom for many".[103]

When you think about it, Jesus is the only man who has ever lived a life of perfect obedience to the Father. Our attempts at morality are completely inadequate, but Jesus lived an authentic life of love. He is the only person in history who truly did not deserve to die. When he said that he had come "to give his life as a ransom for many", he explained why he was prepared to go to the cross under false charges. He did it because it was the only way the price could be paid for our wrongdoing, so that we could be forgiven.

His disciple Peter wrote that "Christ died for sins once for all, the righteous for the unrighteous, to bring you to God".[104] That word 'righteous' means being 'right with

God' or 'good in God's eyes'. Jesus lived the life that we should have lived. He was the righteous man when all of us have fallen short. We know we are not the people we ought to be. But Jesus came to live a perfect life on our behalf. Then when he died, he did so as an extraordinary gift for sinners like you and me. Peter explains that he died for our sins once and for all. He was the righteous man dying for the unrighteous, so that you and I could come back to God.

When Jesus died, he suffered the agony of being separated from his Father in heaven. God was torn in two, as it were. God was taking on himself the punishment we deserve for our sin. He was making good the damage we had caused, so that he would not have to demand the penalty from us anymore. At great cost to himself, God has provided the way that we can be forgiven by accepting the sacrifice of his own Son in our place.

On judgement day, Jesus will be able to forgive us for everything we've ever done wrong because he has already paid the penalty. Although we have rebelled against his reign, he has paid the price for our wrongdoing. God can look at us as if we'd lived the perfect, obedient life he had always wanted us to live, because Jesus lived it on our behalf. A great exchange has taken place—God looks at Jesus and sees a man who has paid for our sin, but God looks at us and sees a life of perfect obedience.

The amazing implications of Jesus' death were clear even as he was dying, in the conversation he had with the criminal next to him.

The Christian life

Two criminals were crucified with Jesus—one on his right and the other on his left. Luke records the conversation that took place as they were killed:

> One of the criminals who hung there hurled insults at him: "Aren't you the Christ? Save yourself and us!"
>
> But the other criminal rebuked him. "Don't you fear God," he said, "since you are under the same sentence? We are punished justly, for we are getting what our deeds deserve. But this man has done nothing wrong."
>
> Then he said, "Jesus, remember me when you come into your kingdom."
>
> Jesus answered him, "I tell you the truth, today you will be with me in paradise."[105]

The second criminal had realized that Jesus was innocent. He had also realized that he himself was guilty, and he feared God. Clearly, when the time came to meet his maker, this thief knew he could not rely on his own deeds. Like the tax collector in Jesus' story, who beat his breast and asked God for mercy, the thief knew that his only hope was to be rescued.

The thief turned to Jesus and said, "Remember me when you come into your kingdom". Remarkably, even as Jesus died on the cross, the thief recognized who Jesus was—that he was the rightful ruler who was going to have a kingdom. And so the thief asked Jesus to remember him.

It's a cry for mercy from a most helpless case—from a

man with a sinful past who had run out of time, and could not make amends for his crimes even if he wanted to. But Jesus' response shows that the heartfelt cry for mercy was enough: "Today you will be with me in paradise". Jesus knew that in his death he was paying the penalty so that the thief by his side could be counted as righteous by God. No matter that the thief had done wrong, no matter that he had no time left on earth to make amends— Jesus died so that anybody who turns back to him and asks for mercy can find complete forgiveness.

At the cross we see that God is a God of justice. He cannot let wrongdoing go unpunished. But we also see that God is a God of love. He paid the penalty himself, so that we don't have to. It was the only way to satisfy both his love and his justice.

It is a truly remarkable picture. When we look at the cross we see what our maker is really like. At the cross, we see God naked, stripped of his clothes and his dignity, and revealing to the world the true extent of his love and justice. We find out the truth about our God when we see him on a wooden cross outside Jerusalem, dying naked and alone, because there was no other way to have us back.

At the cross, we also learn what it truly means to be a Christian. A Christian is not somebody who acknowledges Jesus but who carries on with their broken cisterns and does not turn back to God. Equally, a Christian is not somebody who recognizes Jesus as ruler and thinks that they can get right with God by obeying religious rules. A Christian is somebody who knows that they are not righteous on their own, but who also knows that they are counted as righteous because Jesus died in their place. Their confidence is not in themselves. Their confidence is in the life Jesus lived and the death Jesus died in their place.

You become a Christian by turning and trusting. You turn away from the things you currently serve, the "broken cisterns", and you turn back to God, the "spring of living water". As we will consider again in our final chapter, this is a massive change. You decide to live for God instead of living for yourself or other things. You accept that Jesus is the rightful, risen ruler of this world, and you decide to submit to him from now on. And as you turn, you trust. You trust in Jesus' promise that he has died in your place so that you can be completely forgiven. You trust that you can turn back to God and be accepted because of Jesus' sacrifice on the cross.

It's worth thinking about what it will be like if you decide to become a Christian. No matter what you have ever done in your life, the slate will be completely wiped clean. You will have no reason to feel guilty before God, because Christ has paid the ransom for you. When God the Father looks at you, he sees his perfect Son Jesus Christ.

With this freedom from guilt will come a feeling of peace with God. You do not need to earn your way into his good books. He loves you so much that he took the punishment for you, so that you can be reconciled to him. You could not have earned this love—it is unconditional love.

God promises that you can be one of his children. He is the perfect Father—ambitious for you to become like

Jesus, wanting you to grow and become the person he always wanted you to be. You can speak to him and know him as a loving Father.

Having God as your Father in this way gives meaning to your work. You now work not just for your boss, but for your heavenly Boss, seeking to live and work in a way that honours and pleases him. And you will not be doing this under any pressure of having to get yourself right with him. You will be doing it because he has already made you right with him out of his own love for you.

Becoming a Christian also gives you an instant family of other people all over the world who also have God as their Father. You won't be a lone ranger as a Christian—God wants you to work together with other Christians, loving one another and sharing whatever gifts you have to offer.

God promises that he will help you to do all of this by actually coming and dwelling within you. God will give you his own Spirit—sometimes called the 'Holy Spirit' in the Bible—to help you to become the person God wants you to be. And when you mess up and feel unworthy, the Spirit will remind you that you are still a forgiven child of God because your status doesn't depend on your own performance.

I have sometimes heard people say that Christianity is "not really for me". Now I can understand why formal old cathedrals with long services might not really be for you. And I fully sympathize with the idea that over-sentimental Christian music with tambourines and rainbow guitar straps might not really be for you. But real Christianity is literally what you were made for. It's what all of us were made for.

And real Christianity is only possible because Jesus Christ died for people like you and me. The love that God showed for us on the cross can transform your life. The change will begin the day you put your trust in Jesus Christ.

But for the thief on the cross, the day he put his trust in Jesus was the day he died. When he asked Jesus to remember him, he knew he wouldn't live to enjoy the benefits in this life. Yet Jesus promised him paradise. In our next chapter, we will consider what that paradise will be like.

CHAPTER 14

WHERE WE'RE HEADING

I F SONGWRITERS CAPTURE THE FEELINGS OF OUR times, then it's fair to say that heaven isn't something we find attractive. In 2008, *Mike Skinner and The Streets* released 'Heaven for the weather', in which he sang, "I want to go to heaven for the weather, but hell for the company; I want to go to heaven for the weather, but hell seems like fun to me".

Mike Skinner rapped about "the eternal hell of boredom in heaven", and he wasn't the first musician to have a hit on the subject. In Billy Joel's 1977 single, 'Only the good die young', he sang: "They say there's a heaven for those who will wait. Some say it's better but I say it ain't. I'd rather laugh with the sinners than cry with the saints. The sinners are much more fun."

It's no wonder that this is how we feel when the images

we have about heaven are so miserable. Who wants to spend forever and ever in a place of harps and fluffy clouds, where everybody is painfully boring and you have to wear white? If that's really what heaven is like, then perhaps the weather will be its only redeeming feature.

The problem is that these clichéd images of heaven bear very little resemblance to what Jesus taught about the life to come. In the last chapter, we heard about the thief on the cross who asked to be remembered in Jesus' kingdom. Jesus promised him 'paradise'. What did Jesus mean by that?

Jesus was once a dinner guest at the house of a religious man, and he urged his host and the other guests to show hospitality to people who could not repay it themselves. He referred to "the resurrection of the righteous",[106] when people will be repaid for showing such generosity. Afterwards, he gave a fascinating insight into how things will be for us after we die.

> When one of those at the table with him heard this, he said to Jesus, "Blessed is the man who will eat at the feast in the kingdom of God."
>   Jesus replied: "A certain man was preparing a great banquet and invited many guests. At the time of the banquet he sent his servant to tell those who had been invited, 'Come, for everything is now ready.'"[107]

One of Jesus' dinner companions says how great it will be to feast in "the kingdom of God"—which was a way of referring to the world to come, or eternity, or whatever we want to call what comes next after this life. According to Jesus, this "kingdom of God" will not be all clouds and white nighties, with harps and choirs and nothing to do. It will be like a great banquet.

You can picture a feast being prepared with all of your favourite food, course after course. The finest chefs have been hired, and the finest wine has been selected. It's the greatest feast you could dream of. And of course, a great banquet is not just about the food. It's also about enjoying a memorable evening with other people. It's a celebration. You enjoy it because you're there with friends, sharing the experience and laughing together. The conversation is free-flowing and the banter is unbeatable.

This is the picture Jesus gives us of what heaven will be like, and it fits in with everything else he taught about it throughout his life. It's a picture of richness, abundance, feasting, enjoyment, good company, laughter and celebration.

And did you notice that it's a very *physical* sort of description. This helps correct a very widely held mis-understanding. The next world is not going to be full of ghosts or spirits who sit on clouds. We must remember that God created the real, physical universe we live in now, and he's not going to give up on it. At the moment, the world is not in the state it should be, and that's because we're not the people we should be. But Jesus promised that when he comes on that day of judgement, he will renew the world. He will make everything better.

In fact, it fits much better to talk about a 'new creation' as the place we're heading for, rather than the more ethereal sounding 'heaven'. The new creation (or what the Bible sometimes calls "a new heaven and a new earth") will be something like our world now, but with everything and everyone in it put right. It's as if the world we're in now is just a shadow, and God's kingdom, the new creation, is the real thing around the corner.

The new creation will be a real place, and we will have real bodies. Just as Jesus rose again after he died, we will rise again and live and work and rest in his perfect new world. But things will be different, because we won't die again. The last book of the Bible looks to the future and gives us this breathtaking image of what the new creation will be like:

> Then I saw a new heaven and a new earth, for the first heaven and the first earth had passed away, and there was no longer any sea. I saw the Holy City, the new Jerusalem, coming down out of heaven from God, prepared as a bride beautifully dressed for her husband. And I heard a loud voice from the throne saying, "Now the dwelling of God is with men, and he will live with them. They will be his people, and God himself will be with them and be their God. He will wipe every tear from their eyes. There will be no more death or mourning or crying or pain, for the old order of things has passed away."[108]

This is an extraordinary promise, because it is exactly the world that we all want. If you were asked to describe the perfect world, you'd take away the death and the suffering and the sadness. In fact, we often wonder why God doesn't do that. But Jesus promised that God will do it—that in his kingdom, all of the sadness will be taken away. It's a truly wonderful promise.

But that's not even the best part. The absolute high-light of the new creation is that God will be there. In one sense, God is in this world now, involved in our lives. In the new creation, though, God will be with us far more profoundly than he is now. He will live with us, and we will be his people, and he will be our God. It's a picture of greater intimacy, where God is in the place he should be and we enjoy living under his loving rule and blessing.

How could this be possible, given the way we are? If God's kingdom is going to be a wonderful new creation in which nobody is ever hurt, then how could we possibly live there without spoiling it? We all have our moments. We've all hurt people's feelings before, and we'll do the same again. If we're going to be in the new creation, and God is going to live with us, then there will need to be some major changes.

And that is exactly what is promised. Jesus promises that when we live with him in the world to come, he will change us by his Spirit so that we will be like him. Just think about what that will be like. Jesus will be there with us—the greatest person who ever lived, the man with such a unique, unparalleled character of love and humility—

and we will see him and know him face to face. And God promises that in the new creation our hearts will be transformed so that we will be like Jesus.

He will be the Son of God, and we will be his brothers and sisters. He will be the king, and we will reign with him. We won't spoil everything, because God will change us into the people he always wanted us to be. It's not a personality transplant. You'll still be you and I'll still be me. But we'll be ourselves more fully than we've ever been before, because God will put us right.

The new creation will be real and physical, full of brilliant people put right by God, and Jesus himself will be there with us. What's more, it will never end. The enjoyment will go on forever.

This is what Jesus promised. It's a hope that you can have for yourself if you trust in him. But his parable that day about the great banquet didn't stop there. When we pick up the story again, we find a cutting twist after the master of the house sent his servant to tell the invited guests that the banquet was ready.

> "But they all alike began to make excuses. The first said, 'I have just bought a field, and I must go and see it. Please excuse me.'
>
> "Another said, 'I have just bought five yoke of oxen, and I'm on my way to try them out. Please excuse me.'
>
> "Still another said, 'I just got married, so I can't come.'

"The servant came back and reported this to his master. Then the owner of the house became angry and ordered his servant, 'Go out quickly into the streets and alleys of the town and bring in the poor, the crippled, the blind and the lame.'

"'Sir,' the servant said, 'what you ordered has been done, but there is still room.'

"Then the master told his servant, 'Go out to the roads and country lanes and make them come in, so that my house will be full. I tell you, not one of those men who were invited will get a taste of my banquet.'"[109]

The twist is that some people will refuse to come to the party. In the story, where God is the host, and the guests represent people like you and me, Jesus explains that some people will turn down the chance to be at the banquet.

The invited guests make their excuses. One of them is distracted by his land. He would rather go and see his new field than go to the feast. The second guest has his business interests to take care of. He wants to try out his new oxen. The third guest is distracted by his relationship. He just got married, so it's not a good time.

Of course, these are all terribly lame excuses. They all knew about the banquet in advance, and could easily have made time to come. The various things they needed to do instead could all have waited. The reality is that they just didn't want to be with the host.

It's the same for us. God has invited us to his great

banquet, but many of us make excuses. It might be our career that gets in the way, or our leisure or our relationships. It might be that we make intellectual excuses to keep God at a distance, even though we have seen compelling evidence that Jesus' claims were true. But whatever the reasons, the result is that the host of the party is snubbed. We decline the invitation because we don't want to spend time with him.

And then we have the host's reaction. He is rightly angry, and resolves that the original people he invited will not be allowed to come. The story has a horrible sting in the tail. Jesus will exclude people from the banquet of his kingdom.

When the story is considered from the host's point of view, God's position is understandable. He has offered us life as it was meant to be, as the spring of living water. But we have rejected him and turned to broken cisterns instead. And so, at great cost to himself, God sent Jesus to pay the penalty so that we could turn back to him. Yet many people who hear this message still make lame excuses and decline the invitation. We can't blame God for being indignant, and for excluding people from his banquet.

Being excluded from the banquet is what Jesus elsewhere called 'hell'. Just as we need to re-examine what we think about 'heaven' and appreciate the new creation that's really on offer, we also need to remove our preconceptions about hell and understand what Jesus meant by it.

Jesus taught frequently about the place he called 'hell' —more than anyone else in the Bible in fact. Just as the images Jesus used to describe the new creation emphasized richness, feasting, joy, good company, and so on, so his descriptions of 'hell' focus on the absence of all that is good. This is because God is profoundly absent from hell, and God is the source of all that is good. To be in hell, is to be excluded from all the good gifts that God gives. So hell won't be full of richness and feasting, or joy and laughter, or relationships with loved ones. Hell will be loneliness and pain and an eternal regret for having spurned God's goodness. In Jesus' parable about Lazarus, who lies poverty-stricken, miserable and uncared for at a rich man's gate, the rich man ends up in hell—it is a place of fire and torment, where he longs for relief.[110]

All of this is very confronting, but Jesus intended it to be. When Jesus finally judges the world, he will hold everybody to account for the way they have lived. Justice will be done, and every wrong paid for. Out of his love for everyone who has ever suffered pain, God will not allow anyone to get away with sin.

But we also cannot avoid the fact that, as Solzhenitsyn wrote, "the line dividing good and evil cuts through the heart of every human being". There are no exceptions. On our own, we all face a guilty verdict. On our own, we all face hell.

The marvellous news, of course, is that Jesus came to pay the penalty for our sin so that we don't have to. He came so that we could be free to enter the great banquet and enjoy God's riches for ever. But the truth is that if we decline his invitation, we will be left to pay the penalty ourselves. This is miserable, but it's the right and unavoidable consequence of choosing to live our life separated from God. When we die, God will affirm our decision to reject him. Hell will be awful, and Jesus died so that we can avoid it.

So what about the banquet that the invited guests rejected? Jesus continued in the story by explaining what the host did next. He invited the poor, the crippled, the blind and the lame. When they had come, the host still had room. And so he invited still more of them, from far and wide, so that his house was full for the banquet.

The Bible says that people will be at the great banquet from every tribe and tongue and nation. This might have seemed an extremely bold claim in Jesus' time, but today we can already see it happening. While many people around us in the affluent West are rejecting their invitation, in Africa, China and Latin America people are turning to Jesus Christ in their droves. The party will happen, whether or not we accept our invitation.

In his story, Jesus refers to the poor and the lame. These were the kind of people his audience would have considered least likely to be found in the kingdom of God. His point is that his invitation goes out to everyone, no matter how unlikely a guest they might seem.

And this is great news for you and me. God is throwing the most amazing party we could ever imagine, and Jesus is asking us to accept the invitation. You might think that you're the most unlikely guest, and that the invitation just isn't for you, but Jesus says you must come. He wants you to be there. It doesn't matter if you've never been to church in your life. It doesn't matter how bad you've been. It doesn't matter what your parents believe. It doesn't matter what nationality you are. Jesus wants you there.

It doesn't matter if you've lived your whole life as a Muslim or a Hindu or an atheist. It doesn't matter what other people think of you. It doesn't matter if you were given this book by a Christian friend, and you're only reading it to keep them off your back. Jesus invites you to accept his invitation and come to the banquet. He's paid the price with his life, so that you can be invited to his new creation.

This is why Jesus came. In the life he lived and the death he died, he paid the ransom so that we can turn back to God. When we examine the stark contrast between these destinations, the gift Jesus offers us through his death on the cross becomes all the more wonderful. What we have seen in this chapter is that nothing in this world is more important than our response to this. We must accept the invitation, before it's too late. In our final chapter, we will consider the choice that we all face.

CHAPTER 15

NAKED CHOICE

The free ticket

Exam time at Cambridge was always full-on. But once it was over, there were some equally full-on celebrations, including expensive balls that went on through the night and into the morning. The parties were elaborate, and expensive. They lasted for nine hours, with great food and free drinks everywhere. Famous bands and headline DJs provided music in different marquees, and the old college courtyards were filled with bars and activities.

One evening, I decided to try and gatecrash one of these balls. I wasn't a Christian at the time. Anyway, it turned out that I wasn't the only one who'd had the idea. While people inside were having the time of their lives, the old college buildings were surrounded by young men and women in their dinner suits and dresses, all climbing over walls and hedges in the dark, trying to sneak in and join the fun.

After trying for a while without success, I decided to call it a night. On my way home, though, I had some incredible good fortune. I bumped into the members of a band that had been performing at the ball. They were dropping off their instruments in a van before heading back in to enjoy the rest of the party. I got chatting to them, and it turned out that one of them was going straight home. When he realized that I had been trying to get in, he did a most generous thing. He gave me his badge, which said, 'Performer'. The badge entitled its wearer to go back into the ball as part of the payment for their gig.

I put on the badge and walked straight through the front door. Security were happy to let me in, because I was wearing the 'Performer' badge. I had swapped places with the real performer, and inside, it was amazing. I'd never been to a party like it before. I found my friends in there, and we enjoyed a fantastic night. The entertainment, the food, the drink, the atmosphere—it was a brilliant experience.

I got all of that because the performer gave me his rights to go in. I couldn't afford a ticket, but the performer had earned himself access and he passed it on to me. This is a fitting illustration of what Jesus did for you and me.

On our own, we cannot put right the damage we have done to our relationship with God. But Jesus lived the perfect life—he is the performer who has earned the right to go to the ball. He offers us his badge. If we take his badge and put it on, we will have no problem being accepted.

When God looks at us and the lives we have lived, he will see Jesus' perfect performance instead.

If you take Jesus up on his offer, I can assure you that it is truly amazing at the ball. Turning back to God means turning back to the relationship we were made for. He is the fountain of living waters, and he made us to enjoy our lives knowing him and honouring him. Nine years ago, when I was at law school, I decided to accept the offer. It really has been completely brilliant so far. There has not been a single day since then that I've regretted putting my trust in Jesus Christ.

It will be amazing from the first day you accept his invitation. You can know God, and enjoy the peace of being completely forgiven. He will be your Father, and you can live your life with meaning and purpose. You can become the person God wants you to be. If you would like to, you can do that today.

And we have also seen that it will be amazing forever. You can look forward to the new creation, when this world will be put right by God and be the place we all want it to be. You can go to the great banquet that Jesus promised. It will be as good as things can possibly get.

In a sense, then, we stand where I did when I met that performer outside the ball. He offered his badge to me, and I had a choice to make. I could go into the ball, or I could reject the invitation.

As we come to the end of this book, I want to urge you to accept the invitation of Jesus Christ and turn back to God.

I hope this book has moved you closer to accepting

Jesus, but you might still have some unanswered questions or issues. If that's the case, then it might be helpful to ask yourself, "What is it that is stopping me from becoming a Christian?" Is there something in your life that is holding you back? Given what we have considered in this book, I hope you will agree there is nothing in this world so valuable that it should get in the way of turning back to God. Jesus said himself, "What good is it for a man to gain the whole world, yet forfeit his soul?"[111]

All the same, you might still have a particular outstanding question, or some further thinking that you need to do. If this is the case, please continue to investigate. We have seen that Jesus' claims are simply too important, and the evidence too compelling, for any of us simply to ignore him, or put things off. One extremely helpful way to follow things up would be to attend a course at a church going through the basics of Christianity.

Then again, you might feel that, having read this book, you have seen and heard enough. You have become convinced about who Jesus was and is, and you would like to know him as your saviour and ruler. You understand that he died for you, and you want to turn back to him and live for him from now on. As we come to the end of *Naked God*, we will consider how you could do that today.

The lost coin

When Jesus made his great offer of forgiveness for all who turn to him, it did not go down well with the proud, self-righteous religious people of his day. They thought, mistakenly, that they could earn God's favour themselves, and so the idea of a free gift of salvation offended them. In order to emphasize what it really means to turn back to God, Jesus told them this parable:

> "Or suppose a woman has ten silver coins and loses one. Does she not light a lamp, sweep the house and search carefully until she finds it? And when she finds it, she calls her friends and neighbours together and says, 'Rejoice with me; I have found my lost coin.' In the same way, I tell you, there is rejoicing in the presence of the angels of God over one sinner who repents."[112]

In the parable, God is like a woman who has lost something of incredible value. I don't know whether you ever lose your valuables. It happens to me all of the time. It is an awful feeling when you think you have lost something important—your mobile phone with all the numbers in it, your keys that would all need to be re-cut, your wallet with all the different cards that would need to be cancelled. When I think I've lost something of value like that, I turn my flat upside down in a frantic search.

Jesus says that is how God feels about you. He has lost you, and he wants you back. You belong to God just as that coin belonged to the woman. You are valuable to him just as that coin was to her. She went to great trouble to find the coin, and we have already seen the measures that God has taken to bring you back to him.

If you have ever lost anything valuable, and then found it, do you remember how good it feels? I absolutely love the feeling. I am so relieved to have found what was lost. The feeling is so good that sometimes I'm almost glad I lost it because it's so nice to get it back again.

Jesus says that God rejoices like that whenever somebody repents. If you ask people to describe what God is like, you'll get lots of different ideas. Not many people, though, will describe God as happy. Yet that is how Jesus described him. God is the host of the great banquet, who rejoices about who is there. He is so happy when one person repents, that he celebrates. That is how he would feel if you were to repent.

'Repenting' is how we accept the invitation. The very first words Jesus speaks in Mark's Gospel are: "The time has come. The kingdom of God is near. *Repent and believe the good news!*"[113] We'll come to back to what "believe the good news" means, but first let's consider what repenting is about.

To repent simply means to turn around. We need to turn around because, by ourselves, we live with our backs turned on God. We choose to live for other things, and refuse to accept God as our maker and ruler. We rely on our broken cisterns, and ignore the ruler who promises us streams of living water.

Repenting means turning back to God. We need to accept that we are living in his world, and that we belong to him. We must resolve that from now on, we will live under his authority. To repent is to submit to Jesus, the risen ruler, instead of going our own way.

This image of turning back is helpful because it reveals something very important about becoming a Christian. When you accept God's invitation, you 're-face' yourself, but you don't replace yourself. There is no need to be put off becoming a Christian because you don't want to be exactly like the Christians you know. God has made us all different, and he doesn't want you to lose your own, unique personality. Rather, he wants you to change the way you're facing. He wants you to turn around and face him instead of facing other things. God doesn't want you to become somebody different, but he wants you to change by living for him.

That's what repentance means, and to "believe the good news" simply means to trust Jesus. As you turn back to God, you do so by trusting that Jesus was indeed the ruler and saviour he claimed to be, and that his death has paid the penalty so that you can be forgiven. Repentance and faith are part of the same act—as you turn away from other things, turn back to God, and trust in Jesus' life and death for you.

Re-facing yourself will inevitably involve changes in your life. It means accepting that Jesus is the risen and rightful ruler. It involves saying sorry to God for the ways in which you've disobeyed him in your life. You will inevitably find that you need to make changes to your lifestyle that you wouldn't otherwise want to make—but that you are now glad to make because you trust in Jesus as the good and wise ruler.

There is no avoiding the fact that accepting God's

invitation is a difficult decision for people like us. We all like the idea of being autonomous and independent, answerable to nobody but ourselves. Yet Jesus commands us to accept his authority. Instead of living for ourselves, he calls us to live for him.

There will be costs that come with turning back to God. You might find that you have family or friends who are upset or even angry at your decision, and that your relationship with them becomes damaged or difficult. You will face opposition for what you believe, and it can take courage to stick to your guns.

Yet all of these changes will be emphatically for our good. We can certainly trust that Jesus wants what's best for us because he died for us. God is ambitious for us to become more like Jesus, and it is a delight to make changes because he has already paid the ransom and adopted us into his family. We don't have to live a certain way to get right with him. Jesus died so that we could get right with him. But we do live a new life as a result, both out of gratitude for what he has done for us and out of recognition that he is the real ruler, not us.

Repentance and trust—that's how we accept the invitation. If you are ready to make that choice, then the first person to talk to about it is God. You do it by speaking to him. Here are the words of a prayer that you might use to do that. Introduce yourself first, if you like, although he already knows who you are.

Heavenly Father,

I know that I have not put you first in my life. I've not lived the way that I should have lived. I am sorry.

But now I repent. Thank you that Jesus died on the cross in my place. I now accept that gift, and trust in him so that I can be forgiven.

Please come into my life by your Holy Spirit, and help me to live for Jesus on earth, until I can be with him forever in your kingdom.

Amen.

If you have prayed that prayer, then you have become a Christian. Things might not feel any different, but we have seen the promises that Jesus made. You stand completely forgiven by God. The slate is wiped clean, your status has changed, and you can rest assured that you have peace with God as your Creator and loving Father.

You will need to think more about what living as a Christian will involve. The first vital step will be to start reading the Bible for yourself—there's simply no better way to get to know God. As you read the Bible, God will teach you about his character, his will, his promises, his plans and purposes for the world, and what it means to live as a Christian. The second vital step will be to start going to a church, because being a Christian isn't something you do on your own. At church you will get to know other Christians and live for God together with them.

At the very beginning of *Naked God*, we looked at the

184 · NAKED GOD

changes that are going on in the world. As we have uncovered the truth about life without God, and then uncovered the truth about Jesus, my hope is that a new change has taken place. I hope that by examining the evidence, you have changed your mind about who Jesus is.

In a changing world, your decision to repent will lead to amazing, exciting changes in your life. But as we finish, we should also spare a thought for the change in heaven. For Jesus promised that if you have repented, then God is rejoicing.

FURTHER READING

About the reliability and historicity of the Bible

- A short booklet that deals succinctly with the issues: Andrew Errington, *Can we trust what the Gospels say about Jesus?*, Matthias Media, Sydney, 2009.
- For a little more detail: John Dickson, *The Christ Files*, Blue Bottle Books, Sydney, 2006.
- For those who want to dig into the evidence in greater depth: Craig Blomberg, *The Historical Reliability of the Gospels*, rev. edn, IVP Academic, Downers Grove, 2007.

About the questions and objections people have to Christianity

Timothy Keller, *The Reason for God: Belief in an Age of Scepticism*, Hodder & Stoughton, London, 2008.

About the Christian life

For those who have decided to become a Christian, or are seriously thinking about it: Paul Grimmond, *Right Side Up*, Matthias Media, Sydney, 2009.

ENDNOTES

1 Barack Obama, 2008 USA election victory speech, Chicago, 4 November 2008: www.telegraph.co.uk/news/worldnews/northamerica/usa/barack obama/3383581/Barack-Obamas-victory-speech-Full-text.html

2 Antony Flew, 'Flew Speaks Out: Professor Antony Flew reviews the God Delusion', UCCF: The Christian Union, Leicester, 2008: www.bethinking. org/science-christianity/intermediate/flew-speaks-out-professor-antony-flew-reviews-the-god-delusion.htm

3 Richard Dawkins, *The God Delusion*, Black Swan, London, 2007, pp. 32-3.

4 'Affluence: Happiness (and how to measure it)', *The Economist*, 23 December 2006, p. 13.

5 Alister McGrath, *Intellectuals Don't Need God and Other Modern Myths*, Zondervan, Grand Rapids, 1993, p. 15.

6 Dawkins, *River Out of Eden: A Darwinian View of Life*, Phoenix, London, 1996, pp. 154-5.

7 Dawkins, *The God Delusion*, p. 126.

8 Friedrich Nietzsche, *Human, All Too Human*, trans. Marion Farber, University of Nebraska Press, Lincoln, 1984, no. 106, p. 74, cited in James W Sire, *The Universe Next Door*, 4th edn, IVP, Downers Grove, 2004, p. 91.

9 Charles Darwin, in a letter to W Graham, 3 July 1881, cited in *The Autobiography of Charles Darwin and Selected Letters*, Dover, New York, 1958 (1892), cited in Sire, p. 98.

10 Sire, p. 100.

11 Dawkins, 'The Simple Answer: Nick Pollard talks to Dr. Richard Dawkins', *Third Way*, April 1995, vol. 18, no. 3, cited in 'Atheism and Child Abuse', The Damaris Trust, Southampton: www.damaris.org/content/content.php ?type=5&id=166

12 Ravi Zacharias, *Can Man Live Without God*, W Publishing, Nashville, 1994, p. 21.

13 Viktor Frankl, *The Doctor and the Soul: Introduction to Logotherapy*, Knopf, New York, 1982, p. xxi, cited in Zacharias, p. 25.

14 Zacharias, pp. 27, 32.

15 Sire, p. 107.

16 Martin Luther King, Jr., 'I have a dream', Washington D.C., 28 August 1963: www.americanrhetoric.com/speeches/mlkihaveadream.htm

17 Timothy George, 'Why we still need Moody', *Christianity Today*, 6 December 1999: www.christianitytoday.com/ct/1999/december6/9te066.html

18 Dr Denis Alexander, 'Is it possible to be a Christian and believe in evolution?', UCCF: The Christian Unions, Leicester: www.bethinking.org/resource.php?ID=178&TopicID=2&CategoryID=1

19 Dr Francis Collins, Interview with Bob Abernethy, *Religion & Ethics Newsweekly*, television program, PBS, Washington D.C., 2000: www.pbs.org/wnet/religionandethics/transcripts/collins.html

20 Stephen Jay Gould, 'Impeaching a Self-Appointed Judge', *Scientific American*, vol. 267, no. 1, July 1992, pp. 118-21, cited in Alister McGrath, *The Dawkins Delusion?*, IVP, Leicester, 2007, p. 34.

21 Papias, in around 130 AD, reported this connection between Mark and Peter, writing, "Mark became Peter's interpreter and wrote accurately all that he remembered" (Papias, cited in Eusebius, *Ecclesiastical History* 3.39.15, trans. Kirsopp Lake, Loeb Classical Library, vol. 153, Harvard University Press, Cambridge, 1926, p. 297).

22 Luke 1:3

23 Mark 4:38

24 John 21:11

25 Luke 3:1-2

26 R Bauckham, *Jesus and the Eyewitnesses: the Gospels as Eyewitness Testimony*, Eerdmans, Grand Rapids, 2006.

27 LD Reynolds, *Texts and Transmission: A Survey of the Latin Classics*, Clarendon Press, Oxford, 1983, cited in Rico Tice, *Christianity Explored Study Guide*, The Good Book Company, Surrey, 2005, p. 4.

28 Josh McDowell Ministry, 'Hasn't the New Testament been changed?', UCCF: The Christian Unions, Leicester: www.bethinking.org/bible-jesus/q-hasnt-the-new-testament-been-changed.htm; and Dr Norman Geisler, 'The Dating of the New Testament', UCCF: The Christian Unions, Leicester: www.bethinking.org/bible-jesus/the-dating-of-the-new-testament.htm

29 Frederic G Kenyon, *The Bible and Archaeology*, Harper & Row, New York, 1940, pp. 288-9, cited in Josh McDowell Ministry, 'Hasn't the New Testament been Changed?'

30 Josephus, *Antiquities of the Jews* 18.63-64, in *Josephus: The Complete Works*, trans. W Whiston, Thomas Nelson, Nashville, 1998, p. 576; and Tacitus, *Annals of Imperial Rome* 15.44, trans. John Jackson, Loeb Classical Library, vol. 322, Harvard University Press, Cambridge, 1937, p. 283.

31 Mark 4:41

32 Luke 5:20-21

33 Luke 9:9

34 Brian Macarthur (ed.), *The Penguin Book of Historic Speeches*, Penguin, London, 1996, p. 23.

35 e.g. Mark 1:27

36 Luke 4:17-21

37 John 5:39-40

38 John 10:30-33

39 Matthew 11:28

40 John 8:12

41 Luke 5:20; Matthew 7:21-23

42 John 7:37-38

43 CS Lewis, *Mere Christianity*, HarperCollins, New York, 2001, p. 52.

44 Dawkins, *The God Delusion*, p. 92.

45 *Good Will Hunting*, motion picture, Be Gentlemen Limited Partnership, Boston, 1997. Distributed by Miramax and starring Matt Damon and Ben Affleck.

46 Quoted in Philip Yancey, *The Jesus I Never Knew*, HarperCollins, London, 1995, p. 81.

47 Luke 5:1-11

48 Luke 5:27-31

49 Mark 5:21-24a

50 Mark 1:38

51 Mark 5:24b-34

52 Luke 5:30, 7:39

53 John 13:3-5

54 Luke 23:33-34a

55 Matthew 28:18

56 Luke 6:17-18a

57 Luke 6:27-36

58 Luke 8:5-8
59 Luke 8:11-15
60 Luke 6:27; Mark 12:31; Matthew 5:9, 7:12; John 15:13
61 John 6:28-29
62 John 14:23
63 Jeremiah 23:5; Luke 3:23, 31
64 Micah 5:2; Matthew 2:1
65 Jeremiah 31:15; Matthew 2:16-18
66 Hosea 11:1; Matthew 2:14-15
67 Isaiah 40:3; Matthew 3:1-3; Luke 3:16
68 Isaiah 9:1; Matthew 4:12-17
69 Zechariah 9:9; Luke 19:35-37
70 Josh McDowell, *Evidence That Demands a Verdict*, Thomas Nelson, Nashville, 1999, pp. 183-92. The rest of this chapter contains selected references from *Evidence That Demands a Verdict*, pp. 164-202.
71 Psalm 41:9 fulfilled in Matthew 10:4; Zechariah 11:12 fulfilled in Matthew 26:15; Zechariah 11:13 fulfilled in Matthew 27:5-7; Zechariah 13:7 fulfilled in Matthew 26:31, 51-56; Psalm 35:11 fulfilled in Matthew 26:59-60; Isaiah 53:7 fulfilled in Matthew 27:12; Isaiah 53:5 fulfilled in Matthew 27:26; Isaiah 50:6 fulfilled in Matthew 26:67; Psalm 22:7-8 fulfilled in Matthew 27:29; Psalm 22:16 fulfilled in Luke 23:33; Isaiah 53:12 fulfilled in Matthew 27:38 and in Luke 23:34; Psalm 22:17 fulfilled in Luke 23:35; Psalm 109:25 fulfilled in Matthew 27:39; Psalm 22:18 fulfilled in John 19:23-24; Zechariah 12:10 fulfilled in John 19:34; Psalm 34:20 fulfilled in John 19:33.
72 John 20:30-31
73 Luke 5:20
74 Luke 5:22-26
75 CS Lewis, *Miracles*, HarperCollins, New York, 2001, p. 75.
76 Luke 8:25
77 Mark 8:27-29
78 CS Lewis, *Miracles*, pp. 212-13.
79 Lee Strobel, *The Case for Christ*, Zondervan, Grand Rapids, 1998, p. 199.
80 Mark 16:1-3
81 Mark 16:4-8
82 Josephus, *Antiquities of the Jews* 4.219, in *Josephus: The Complete Works*, p. 139.
83 1 Corinthians 15:3-6
84 Luke 24, especially verse 43.

85 John 20:25

86 John 20:26-29

87 Pinchas Lapide, *The Resurrection of Jesus: A Jewish Perspective*, trans. Wilhelm C Linss, Augsburg Publishing, Minneapolis, 1983, p. 125.

88 Michael Green, *Man Alive*, IVP, Leicester, 1968, cited in Nicky Gumbel, *Questions of Life*, 2nd edn, Kingsway, Eastbourne, 1995, p. 43.

89 John 11:25-26

90 Acts 17:30-31

91 Gary A Haugen, *Good News About Injustice*, IVP, Downers Grove, 1999, p. 85.

92 Timothy Keller, *The Reason for God: Belief in an Age of Scepticism*, Hodder and Stoughton, London, 2008.

93 Marie Chapian, *Of Whom the World was not Worthy*, Bethany, Minneapolis, 1978, pp. 122-3, cited in Zacharias, 'The Touch of Truth', in DA Carson (ed.), *Telling the Truth*, Zondervan, Grand Rapids, 2000, p. 42.

94 John 8:31-36

95 Jeremiah 2:13

96 John 7:37-38

97 The use of this scene as an illustration is courtesy of Charlie Skrine, St Helen's Church, Bishopsgate, London.

98 Luke 12:1-3

99 Alexandra Solzhenitsyn, *Gulag Archipelago 1918-1956: An Experiment in Literary Investigation*, abridged, trans. Thomas P Whitney and Harry Willetts, Harper Perennial, 2002, p. 75.

100 Mark 2:17

101 Luke 18:9-14

102 Mark 8:31

103 Mark 10:45

104 1 Peter 3:18

105 Luke 23:39-43

106 Luke 14:14

107 Luke 14:15-17

108 Revelation 21:1-4

109 Luke 14:18-24

110 Luke 16:19-31

111 Mark 8:36

112 Luke 15:8-10

113 Mark 1:15

ACKNOWLEDGEMENTS

I WANT TO THANK TONY PAYNE. WITHOUT HIS encouragement and brilliant editing, this book would never have become a reality.

Thanks to Ed Drew, Mark Fossey, Andy Mason and Hugh Mawby for their help with and enthusiasm for the project. Thanks to Nigel Beynon and Tim Keller, whose thoughts have helped to shape my own on a number of the issues covered in this book. And above all, thanks to Cathy for all of her patience and support.

Finally, thanks to the friends from Trinity Hall and Freshfields whose questions about God inspired me to write.

Matthias Media is an independent Christian publishing company based in Sydney, Australia. To browse our online catalogue, access samples and free downloads, and find more information about our resources, visit our website:

www.matthiasmedia.com.au

How to buy our resources

1. Direct from us over the internet:
   – in the US: www.matthiasmedia.com
   – in Australia and the rest of the world:
     www.matthiasmedia.com.au

2. Direct from us by phone:
   – in the US: 1 866 407 4530
   – in Australia: 1800 814 360 (Sydney: 9663 1478)
   – international: +61-2-9663-1478

3. Through a range of outlets in various parts of the world. Visit **www.matthiasmedia.com.au/international.php** for details about recommended retailers in your part of the world, including www.thegoodbook.co.uk in the United Kingdom.

4. Trade enquiries can be addressed to:
   – in the US and Canada: sales@matthiasmedia.com
   – in Australia and the rest of the world:
     sales@matthiasmedia.com.au